ORDINARY MAGIC
A FATHER-SON JOURNEY ON THE COLORADO TRAIL

Todd Fahnestock

Copyright © 2021 Todd Fahnestock

All rights reserved.

No part of this book may be reproduced, or stored in a retrieval system, or transmitted in any form or by any means, electronic, mechanical, photocopying, recording, or otherwise, without express written permission of the publisher.

ISBN 13: 978-1-952699-17-7

Cover design by:
Rashed AlAkroka

Back cover photo by:
A.J. Johnson

For my children,
Who make me proud every day.

CONTENTS

ORDINARY MAGIC

Chapter 1 – Magic Hunter	1
Chapter 2 – Dr. Smiley and Mr. Lizard-Brain	6
Chapter 3 – The Colorado Trail	11
Chapter 4 – Packing	16
Chapter 5 – Beginning the Trail	21
Chapter 6 – Purple Mountains	38
Chapter 7 – The First Night	45
Chapter 8 – Underwear	50
Chapter 9 – Food from the Heavens	55
Chapter 10 – The Great Farting	71
Chapter 11 – Two Dead Rabbits	80
Chapter 12 – Georgia Pass	88
Chapter 13 – Zero Day	93
Chapter 14 – Copper Mountain	108
Chapter 15 – Lightning on Searle Pass	116
Chapter 16 – World War II Bunker	131
Chapter 17 – The Electric Blue Shoes	139
Chapter 18 – Dash's Decision	149

Chapter 19 – My Favorite Moment	155
Chapter 20 – Baldy Lake	162
Chapter 21 – The Long Wait	169
Chapter 22 – Bear Mace to the Face	178
Chapter 23 – River Sirens	188
Chapter 24 – High Country	205
Chapter 25 – The Waterfall	215
Chapter 26 – A Dangerous Shower	226
Chapter 27 – Ordinary Magic	232
Mailing List/Social Media	241
Acknowledgements	243
Author Letter	246
Other Works	248
About the Author	249

Mailing List/Social Media

MAILING LIST
Don't miss out on the latest news and information about all of my books. Join my Readers Group:
https://www.subscribepage.com/u0x4q3

FACEBOOK
https://www.facebook.com/todd.fahnestock

AMAZON AUTHOR PAGE
https://www.amazon.com/Todd-Fahnestock/e/B004N1MILG

ORDINARY MAGIC
A FATHER-SON JOURNEY ON THE COLORADO TRAIL

1
MAGIC HUNTER

I'VE BEEN SEARCHING FOR MAGIC my whole life, I think.

It happened in unconscious ways when I was a child. My imagination was like an extra friend following me around, whispering in my ear, shaping what I saw. I'd search for dinosaurs behind our gold velvet couch. I'd telepathically talk to my dog Sprock and see his reactions the way I wanted to see them, like he was responding to my mental command to run across the back yard or leap atop the stack of pallets my dad had brought home from work. I'd feel cold wafts from the upstairs attic and know it was a place I didn't want to go. There were ebbs and flows to things, energy I felt—or imagined I felt—that I thought everyone could feel.

I was drawn to these moments where imagination and reality blurred together, and I remember trying to explain it to my mom. She watched me and listened, and I felt she understood me. Looking back, I think she just liked the idea of a six-year-old being able to feel magic. But her interest encouraged me; I wanted to stand at the center of that crossroads of reality and imagination. I wanted to be a part of it. I could never have cerebralized it when I was six years old, but I'm convinced now that I was unconsciously looking for magic.

And I remember when I *consciously* chose to look for magic.

I was fourteen, living in Durango, Colorado, and my parents gathered me and my siblings in the dining room. They were getting a divorce, they said. They handed the news to us like we were adults, like a statement of the facts would make us "understand," but I don't remember their reasons. At that age, my rational mind was a fledgling thing with little control over me, whereas my emotions were wild and strong. They galloped like terrified horses, scattering every which way at the news.

My little sister, five years younger than me, just grinned her happy little grin like nothing was wrong. I don't think she understood what was really happening. My older brother seemed to understand just fine, but he came to a conclusion that confounded me.

"Well, it's about time," he said.

That was the opposite of how I felt. I didn't think it was "about time." I mean, I'd sat at this table countless times listening to Top 40 radio while doing my homework or playing D&D with my friends. I'd read Edgar Rice Burroughs's *A Princess of Mars* and Lloyd Alexander's *The Book of Three* in that bay window, which my father had installed himself. I'd been filled with a sense of permanence and contentment here, never once imagining a future that didn't include me growing up in this house with two parents who loved each other.

"Well, I think it sucks," I said, and that's all I said. I got up from the table and ran to my room, imagining the house coming apart around me, all the boards becoming unstuck and floating up into the blue sky until there was just me, running down a hallway with no walls, no ceiling, and nowhere to go.

Two days after my parents dropped the bomb, I stood at the edge of a precipice looking down at the Animas River. I was so scared, and I hated it. I wanted it to stop. I wanted to charge at the fear like it was something tangible, like if I could burst through it, it would go away. I thought about the most frightening thing I could do, something worse than my parents splitting up. I wondered what it would be like to jump.

I wondered what it would be like to die.

I didn't jump, but I still felt like I was falling. It felt like I'd leaned too far back in a chair, right where I should jerk and catch my balance, except I hadn't, but I hadn't hit the floor yet either. That stomach-hollowing, scalp-prickling fear just went on and on.

I stood there at the edge of that cliff, looking across the river, past the beginnings of the little industrial park south of Durango, to the closest foothills and then to the mighty mountains beyond. A whole world. A whole scary world out there, and the reason I felt like I was falling was because I didn't have a safety net anymore. What my brother was ready for at age sixteen—and what my little sister didn't realize at age nine—was that our lives were over. That was what our parents had just told us, really. The magic of our family had been fractured, and it was going to simply come apart in pieces.

I wanted to die. I didn't want to live with this constant fear, didn't want to go back to school. Didn't want to go home. I had nowhere to turn, and I was crawling out of my skin with a need to know what came next. Except there were no answers. There was only that distant, beautiful horizon, and I just kept staring at it.

I finally decided to go to school, decided I'd take just one step and see what happened. It couldn't be worse than this feeling, could it? And if that one step worked out, I'd take another. I resigned myself to do…whatever happened next. One little bit at a time.

And if it all became too much, I promised I'd come back to this place. Not to jump, maybe, but to cross that bridge, walk through that industrial park, start up into those foothills and keep walking until something happened, until the Universe showed me that there was a reason for me to be alive. I'd keep walking until I found something magical, or until I died. That would be my jump instead. That would be my way through the fear—a one-finger salute to the Universe. A dare for Her to do her worst.

That was the first moment I consciously decided to search for magic. It was wrapped up in so many things—the breaking of my family foundation, my wild imagination, the cold fear of a harsh world closing in on me, and the tingling, twisting changes of puberty—but that was the first moment I made a decision to shape the future of my own life. Up to that moment, it had been my parents' job. But obviously they didn't know what they were doing any better than I did. There was no safety net.

I decided two things then.

First, I was going to challenge the Universe. Maybe I wouldn't go walking into the mountains today, but I was going to step into this scary world where nothing was certain and dare it to kill me. I was going to take one step. And if I survived, I'd take another. And those single steps would be the only thing that mattered. I wouldn't look two or ten or twenty steps down the road. Planning for the future was a fiction; my parents had shown me that. I would look only at the one step, and I wasn't going to care about consequences, which meant I could literally do anything.

So I decided to chase the ridiculous. I would search for the magic that had tantalized me all my life. And I didn't mean the "oh, what a magical moment" kind of magic. I wanted fireballs and dragons and telekinesis. I wanted magic that would make others open their mouths in surprise.

My second resolution was: I was never going to have kids. I wouldn't put a child through this. I was never going to offer a safe home and then rip it away. And since I could never guarantee safety even for myself, it was best that I simply never have children.

I was alone now. I was a magic hunter.

The next sixteen years took me on many adventures. I traveled throughout the U.S. and to exotic places halfway around the world. I met good friends and best friends. I took many lovers. And with every step, I looked for that magic I craved.

I never quite found it. I never threw a fireball anywhere except in my own mind. I never moved an object across the room without touching it. I never brushed my hands along the scales of a dragon except in the pages of novels I read or novels I wrote.

In the summer of 2003, I married the love of my life. That winter, I became a father, and in the spring of 2006, we had our second child.

Up until then, I'd been a flighty adventurer prone to leaping into the wind at a moment's notice. I'd never held a job for more than sixteen months. My default setting was to dodge and brush past danger, but this time, hands clasped with my wife, we held that safe home together. I dug in my heels and we created for our children what I had lost so long ago.

This is the story of how, when my son turned the age I had been when my life fell apart, we hiked The Colorado Trail together. It's a story about how I found the magic I'd been looking for. An ordinary magic that had been there all along.

2

DR. SMILEY AND MR. LIZARD-BRAIN

THE WHOLE PLAN BEGAN in April of 2020, a few weeks after my son Dash's 14th birthday. I didn't know about The Colorado Trail yet—didn't even know what it was—but it was looming in my future. I was about to make a pretty crappy dad move, and it would spark a critical realization: I was running out of time with my son. My window to make any *good* dad moves was shrinking.

It literally started with a rude awakening.

I blinked open my eyes. Voices. There were voices in my house. One look at my dark window told me it wasn't morning yet.

Important to note: When I'm jolted out of a dead sleep, I'm not myself. Normally, I'm Dr. Smiley, if you will, chock full of energy and optimism, a cross between Pollyanna and Tigger.

When I'm jolted out of a deep sleep, I'm Mr. Lizard-Brain. There are only enemies in the world, and everything I see is filtered through rage-tinted glasses.

So when those voices jolted me awake, it was Mr. Lizard-

Brain—not Dr. Smiley—who opened his eyes.

Mr. Lizard-Brain told me it was intruders. Someone had broken into my house. I swung upright, put my feet on the cold floor, slid open my nightstand drawer and grabbed my Viking short sword—I collect swords and daggers. It's a weapon with a fourteen-inch blade. It's heavy. It's sharp. And if you're sneaking into my house, it's designed to make a dent in your head.

I crept downstairs. I didn't hear anything. No movement. No sounds of thieving feet creaking across my one-hundred-year-old wooden floors.

Then, the voices came again. Except it wasn't voices; it was just one voice, and this time I recognized it. It was my son.

Except that was impossible. No way it could be *my* son. My kids have a strict ten o'clock bedtime, and it's a school night.

I glided silently through the kitchen, checking the clock as I went. It was three in the morning. I set the Viking short sword on the cutting board, went to Dash's closed door and listened. He was talking to his friend. Talking on the phone.

Mr. Lizard-Brain hissed inside my head, and my shoulders rose like the hackles on an angry dog. He's not supposed to be on his phone after nine o'clock. He knows better!

I burst through his door like The Hulk.

"Dude," I growled. "It's three in the morning!"

Dash jumped in his loft bed. Yes, he was lying down, but he jumped anyway, almost dropped his phone.

I'd already gone through the whole trial in my head, and the verdict had been rendered: guilty. There was no chance for an appeal. "What the hell are you doing?" I demanded.

"Jacob needed me," Dash said.

"Hang up. Now," I demanded.

He hesitated, and Mr. Lizard-Brain swelled to monstrous proportions.

"You hang up, or I'm hanging up for you," I roared. I strode toward his bed, intent on taking his phone and destroying it right in front of him. Mr. Lizard-Brain doesn't care about phones, you see. He doesn't care about psychologically scarring my son. He doesn't care about much of anything except that I'm not asleep and I should be.

"I gotta go," Dash said reluctantly, and he hung up.

"I'm trying to sleep, Dash," I growled. "I'm sleeping, and you're talking like it's daytime. I could hear you upstairs. You woke me up!" I said the last part like I would have said, "You killed the president!"

"He's my friend, Dad. And he needed me," Dash said.

"Not at three o'clock, he doesn't."

"Yes, at three o'clock he did!" Dash pushed back.

"You can't be on the phone with your friend at three in the morning," I growled. "Not ever—"

"And if he needs me," Dash continued, talking over me. "I'm going to help him. I don't care if it's three in the morning. He is just as important to me as you are!"

The statement hit me like a stone. Just as important. *Just* as important.

A collage of Dash and me during the last fourteen years flickered through my mind like an old-time slideshow carousel on speed. Watching him take his first steps. Blowing raspberries on his belly after a bath. Teaching him how to ride a bicycle. Being his fall-block while he climbed a tree or learned to do a back-flip. Sword-fighting with sticks in the backyard. Tickling him until we were both breathless with laughter. Teaching him how to read. Lofting him into our ginormous fall leaf pile.

I clenched my teeth and swallowed. *Just* as important?

But my fatherly sensibilities had finally awoken, and I tried to shove Mr. Lizard-Brain back into his cave. I reminded myself that Dash was not an extension of me and my priorities. As he came closer to adulthood, he was going to make decisions, like who was important in his life. And there was not a damned thing I could do about it.

"Fine," I said through my teeth, trying not to feel the sting. "But not at three in the morning." I held my hand out for his phone.

His lips pressed into a firm line. After a moment's hesitation while Mr. Lizard-Brain—eager to jump back into the fray—hoped Dash would put up a fight, my son slapped the phone into my palm.

"We'll talk more about this in the morning," I said.

I felt his gaze on me like a laser as I left the room.

I had barely crossed the threshold of the doorway when I felt remorse. I'd done that wrong somehow. There had been an opportunity there, a chance to understand, to connect, and in my anger I'd blown right past it.

I have moments like this a lot. I've made some good dad moves in my life, but I've made a lot of bad dad moves, too. It was slowly dawning on me that this was one of the bad ones.

I also had the sense that time had shifted—the very Earth had shifted—and my relationship with my son wasn't the same as it had once been. Somehow I'd blinked and the ten-year-old boy who always wanted to hang out with me, who'd thought I was the best, had vanished. He'd been replaced by this teenage creature who'd just told me that I ranked somewhere below his friend.

I knew the psychology. I knew that the teenage phase is where kids break out of their parent-worshipping mode, where they, in fact, will do anything to prove that they are separate from the parental unit. I understood all that.

But God it hurt like hell.

In the quiet of my kitchen, palms pressed against the butcher block, I paused in sentimental pain, as well as growing remorse, at how I'd handled the situation.

That's when the realization hit me. Not my injured feelings, but something Important with a capital "I." Amidst schedules and work pressures and sleep deprivation and anger, I'd almost missed it.

Dash wasn't going to be a child much longer.

I thought about how quickly I'd shifted from child to adult when I was fourteen, how fast that had happened. My dad hadn't been around for it. I'd had to navigate that on my own. And when I'd finally decided to have kids so many years later,

I'd sworn I would be there for them.

And that moment had come. Now. I felt like I needed to snatch at the open air, to try to catch it before it was gone.

Two days later, I got a call from my friend Megan. And that was when the whole crazy scheme came into focus.

3

THE COLORADO TRAIL

MEGAN AND I HAVE KNOWN each other since college. Our kids—she has an older daughter and a younger son, as do I—are practically the same ages. And they pretty much grew up together because of a yearly camping trip our college friends attend every year.

So I was unsurprised when she called me up one afternoon to shoot the breeze. During the conversation, she mentioned that her sixteen-year-old daughter was thinking about hiking The Colorado Trail.

"The what?" I asked.

"Oh for God's sake, Todd. You live in Colorado. You grew up in Durango. It's The Colorado Trail."

I entertained a dull flicker of recognition in the back of my mind. I mean, I'd heard of the Appalachian Trail because another of my college friends, Lawdon, had hiked it. And it would make sense for there to be something like that here in Colorado, but I had no specific recollection.

"Oh sure! The Colorado Trail!" I faked it enthusiastically. "The one that goes through the mountains."

"You're an idiot," she said.

"It *does* go through the mountains, right?" Practically everything in Colorado goes through the mountains.

She ignored my attempt at humor. Everyone has a different way of dealing with me when I'm acting like an idiot; Megan pretends she doesn't hear me. "So my daughter wants to hike the trail."

"Oh, cool. I can't remember how long that old Colorado Trail is. It's a ways, right?"

"Four hundred and eighty five miles," she said. "Denver to Durango."

"Oh yeah!" I said, snapping my fingers like I'd remembered.

"Just stop," she said.

"Okay."

"Anyway, she's been wanting to hike this trail ever since…well, forever. You know how she goes to that camp every summer in Durango?"

"Yes." *No.*

"Well, they go on a few overnight hikes, some multiple days, and she loves it. Her dream is to thru-hike the CT."

"The CT?"

She paused. If she was religious, I imagine she'd have looked up to God for patience right about now. "Colorado. Trail," she said with exaggerated emphasis.

"Gotcha."

"So she had it all set up to go with her friend, but now the friend can't go and she's really bummed. She can't do it on her own. I mean, I wouldn't let her."

"And her friend is also sixteen?"

"Yes."

"Even that seem s a bit scary. Two teenagers alone in the woods?"

"My daughter knows hiking. She'd be fine, but I'm not okay with her going alone. Now I'm trying to think of someone else who can go with her."

When Megan had mentioned that the trail went from

Denver, where I currently lived, to Durango, where I'd grown up, my imagination started doing its thing. I pictured what it would be like to hike the trail myself, imagined the challenge of it. When she reached her quandary about her daughter's lack of a hiking companion, my response just popped out.

"I'll do it," I said.

She paused. "What?"

"I'll take her on the trail, if you think she'd be okay going with an adult."

"Todd, you're fifty."

That poked my male ego like a hot spear. *Screw you, I'm fifty!* I thought.

"So?" I said, with only a fraction of my annoyance showing.

"So you're *fifty*. This is four hundred and eighty-five miles. Through the mountains. And you're not in shape."

"Hey!"

"Well...you aren't."

"I'm not in *that* bad of shape."

"You're fifty."

When she said that again, I decided I was hiking the Colorado Trail with or without her daughter. And nothing she could say would stop me.

"Well, I'm fourteen at heart," I said in my best nonchalant voice. This is what I do when something scares me, a knee-jerk reaction from that moment at the Animas River. I lower my head and charge right at the fear, which usually leads to me getting in over my head. "Let her know I'd be happy to hike it with her."

"Wow. Well, that's really nice of you. Are you sure?"

A thought formed in my mind. That thing I'd been missing the other night, when I'd railed at Dash at three in the morning, *this* could be the answer.

"Would she mind if Dash went, too?" I asked.

"No! I think she'd love that," Megan said.

"Because if I tell Dash I'm hiking The Colorado Trail, he's going to want to go."

"Perfect," she said.

We chatted for a little while longer, then I hung up and went to find Dash.

As expected, he said, "Hell yes!"

I want to take a moment here to describe my son. You've already seen him at three in the morning when I'm Mr. Lizard-Brain, roaring mad, and he's ready to fight for his friend.

Let me round out the picture.

The Colorado Trail is a whale of an undertaking, a physical test that would have us hiking fifteen miles a day.

Fifteen miles a day. That's more than a half-marathon every day, day after day for five weeks. That's a long way to walk on flat ground over pavement, but we were talking about going up and down thirteen-thousand-foot summits and over ankle-turning rocky trails.

Megan worried that, at age fifty, I might not be able to handle it. One might think the same of a fourteen-year-old boy.

Did I worry Dash wasn't up to the physical challenge? No, I did not. Not for a second.

When Dash was five, he climbed up the drainpipe to the roof of our house, just hand over hand, bare feet gripping the aluminum, smooth and certain. When he reached the rain gutter, he grabbed it with both hands, hung there by his fingers for a moment with a smile, looking around our yard, then muscled himself up as pretty as you please and rolled onto the roof.

He also climbed doorjambs daily—and I'm not talking about pushing against either side of the doorjamb with arms and legs and shimmying up like I did when I was a kid. I'm talking about grabbing one side of the doorjamb like a chip clip and crimping his way up.

When he was ten, he did seven hundred pull-ups in a day. Full, honest-to-God, no-cheating pull-ups.

When he was twelve, after teaching himself how to do backflips, twisting backflips, and full body layouts on the trampoline, he decided he wanted to do a backflip without the trampoline. So he took the guest mattress outside, put it on the lawn, and practiced until he felt he was ready. Then he took away the mattress and did a backflip.

In short, the kid's a beast. I've not seen a physical activity he didn't take to immediately.

So when I suggested The Colorado Trail to him, he said yes in a heartbeat, like I knew he would. The physical part of the trail wasn't going to be a problem for him, that much I knew. The real test would be his attention span and his ability to gut it out through the sucky moments that were sure to arise.

In the end, Megan's daughter didn't go with us. Her own father's schedule unexpectedly opened up for the summer, and he took her instead, nine days ahead of us.

As it turned out, Dash and I would leave on July 13th, on the very last day we could manage it and still get Dash back in time for school. We'd steal out of the city like thieves, racing against time.

4
PACKING

LET'S TALK PACKING.

As you might guess, there are a number of things you need in order to hike for five weeks in the mountains and not die—*not dying* being key to enjoying the experience. And while Dash and I would soon become intimate with terms like *base weight*, *thru-hiking*, *camel up*, *drop points*, *trail angels*, *cowboy camping*, *hiker hunger*, *hot spots*, *Guthook*, and *Zero Days*, I had never heard of any of those things before we started the trail. In the beginning, my mind spun as I just tried to absorb the basics, like food and water and backpacks and hiking boots.

Luckily, Megan's sister had hiked the trail a few years back and, meticulous wonder that she is, had written down not just the list she'd started with, but an amended list after she finished the trail. That amazing little document saved me a lot of legwork. I modified it only slightly for our particular hiking duo.

In no particular order, my final list looked like this:

- Tent

- Waterproof ground cloth
- Rope or cord (for hanging bear bag)
- Bear bag
- Headlamp
- Compass
- Backpack
- Backpack rain cover
- Rain jacket
- Rain pants
- Gloves (lightweight)
- Crocs (for happy camp feet)
- Hiking boots
- Sleeping bag
- Sleeping pad
- Jetboil (never heard of this before the trail; it's the coolest thing ever)
- White gas for Jetboil
- Pot for boiling water
- Spork
- Aqua Mira (or water filter)
- First aid kit
- Sunglasses
- Sunscreen
- Lighter
- Matches
- Pocket knife
- Phone (or sat phone)
- Personal toiletries
- Underwear (wear one, carry one, leave two at home for resupply)
- Short sleeved tech shirt (two to bring, two for resupply)
- Fleece (one to wear, one for resupply)
- Socks (wear one, carry one, two pairs for resupply)
- Puffer jacket (only for the second leg of the journey)
- Cap
- Warm hat

- Hiking pants (one to wear, one for resupply)
- Shorts (one to wear, one for resupply)
- Water bottles
- Drom (large collapsible bottle for carrying water on long sections on the CT that have none)
- Bug spray
- Paper (for fire starting)
- Food, dehydrated (breakfast and dinner)
- Food, not dehydrated (lunches and snacks)
- Tin cups (for boiling dehydrated food)
- Solar charger (totally USELESS; a huge bust)
- Sunscreen lip balm
- Bear mace
- Platypus water filter
- CT Trail Guide
- CT Data book
- Plastic trowel
- Toilet paper

The list made my head swim, but I set about acquiring the items, hoping to have them all together by our intended departure date of July 10th.

So, between Englewood's famous Army Surplus Store (I love that place), Sierra Trading Post, a lovely vegan dehydrated food supplier named Harmony House, and Amazon, I bought the items and checked them off the list and piled them in the corner of my office. By the time I was done, the total came to over one thousand six hundred dollars.

With the final items ordered, I turned my attention from the huge pile of gear to two daunting non-trail tasks I had to get done before my departure: finishing edits on my latest novel, *Summer of the Fetch,* and renovating a bathroom in my ancient house.

When it comes to home repair—when it comes to anything, really—I tend to overreach. I set unreasonable goals, then zip about like The Flash to try to stay on schedule. So I worked like a speed demon on the novel, got that done and out to beta readers, then flipped my attention to the bathroom renovation.

Well, if you've ever done home improvements, you're probably guessing what came next. After ripping out the sink, toilet, cabinets, tile, insulation, all the old galvanized steel plumbing, and the entire floor, stripping the bathroom down to its one-hundred-year-old skeleton, I was already behind schedule, and the rebuilding hadn't even started.

But I soldiered on, installing new pipes and insulation, and reconstructing the entire east wall (which I hadn't planned on—there are always unexpected "gifts" when you do renovations like this). As I was wrestling with Pex pipe, Sharkbite fittings, and the freakin' air vent for the drainpipe, I approached my intended CT departure date of July 10th...and then blew right past it.

With the mounting pressure of needing to get on the trail—not to mention the mounting frustration with myself for biting off more than I could chew—I worked straight through, barely stopping to sleep, until the project was finally done on July 12th.

I was exhausted, but I couldn't rest. If we were going to be able to leave for the trail the next day—already three days behind schedule—I had to get packed. So I focused my attention on the haphazard mountain of gear in my office and started sorting through camping supplies.

I folded up, rolled up, or bagged up all the essentials, then weighed them to establish the "base weight" for my "kit." *Kit* is the term hikers use for items in a pack that don't fluctuate—essentially everything but food and water. *Base weight* is the weight of the kit. The recommended base weight is thirty pounds so that the final pack is fifty pounds or less.

I got my base weight down to twenty-seven pounds, thank you very much.

With the addition of food, water, and some personal items, my final overall pack weighed in at a respectable forty-eight pounds. Dash's was even lighter.

Task complete, I finally breathed a sigh of relief and, not

long after, crashed hard for the night.

I'd like to say that Dash and I got on the trail bright and early the next day, that by at least nine o'clock our boots hit the dirt of Segment 1...

But I would be lying. It didn't happen that way. Already our adventure was about to take a surprise turn.

5
BEGINNING THE TRAIL

WE HADN'T EVEN REACHED the trailhead before we ran afoul of communication issues. My wife Lara was driving, so I wasn't paying attention. I was wrapped up in last-minute business on my phone. With the flurry of action to meet my unreasonable deadlines for *Summer of the Fetch* and the bathroom remodel, I'd neglected all else.

I had to do something about the backlog, otherwise anyone who had business with me would be hanging in limbo for five weeks—with no warning. Almost no one knew I was going to be out of town, hiking the CT. I don't think I really believed it myself until we were in the car.

I hastily set an out-of-office message on my email and texted a few people.

Dash was navigating. I'd passed the job off to him as a sign of faith in our new partnership. We were going to have to start relying on each other, and this seemed a good place to begin.

So we were halfway up Highway 285 before I realized we weren't supposed to be on Highway 285. I raised my head from my phone.

"Trail starts in Waterton Canyon," I said to Lara. "Why are we on Highway 285?"

"This is where you guys told me to go." She glared at me.

"I didn't tell you to go this way," I said.

She rolled her eyes. "Talk to Dash. He's giving me directions."

"I'm going from the book," Dash protested, holding up the thick, heavy Colorado Trail Guide.

"The book says to take 285 to Segment 1?" I asked, dubious. "It starts down by Chatfield."

"Segment 2," Dash said.

"Segment 1," I said. "Is where the trail begins."

"Yeah, and you said Segment 1 sucks and that we were three days behind schedule and that we needed to skip something if we were going to finish on time. You said if we needed to skip a segment, it should be Segment 1. So I skipped it."

I opened my mouth, and then I closed it. He was right. I had said that. A few days ago, while panicked about the bathroom, I'd said that, but since then I'd decided we didn't need to skip it. I'd done the math and figured, if we kept a quick pace, we had just enough time to make it.

Except I hadn't mentioned this to Dash.

"Look," Lara interrupted. "I'll take you wherever you want to go, but you need to decide right now. I've got a meeting at one o'clock that I have to be back in town for. The directions Dash gave me say it's forty-five more minutes to get to Segment 2. We're already cutting it close. You want me to turn around?"

Internally, I railed at the idea of skipping Segment 1, but I calmed myself. This trip wasn't about me. It was about Dash and me. If Dash didn't care, then I wasn't going to let this hiccup spoil the mood. I didn't need to be able to brag to my friends that I hiked "every segment of the Colorado Trail." This was about getting into the wilderness and hiking with my son. And there were still four hundred and seventy miles of trail left. That was plenty of miles.

"Keep going," I said, and I turned to glance at Dash in the back seat. "Good job, buddy. You did what we agreed we'd do. Sorry I got confused."

Half an hour later, we turned off the highway and Lara drove down a long, winding dirt road. She stopped just before a bridge over the South Platte River, the same river that flows through the heart of Denver. The closest town was Conifer, seventeen miles away.

As Dash and I posed with our packs and Lara snapped quick pictures, I began to feel a drop in my stomach. The only evidence of civilization was that bridge over the river, a row of three abandoned shops that looked like they'd been built when Wyatt Earp was still gunslinging, and a squat concrete bathroom, the kind you'd see at an interstate rest stop. There was no cell service here. Once Lara left, there'd be no chance to reach back to her and say, "Wait! Never mind! Come get us!" Our safety net would vanish. We'd have to survive with the items we'd brought along.

I confess, a small part of me wanted to call it quits right then, wanted to hop back into the safety of the car, go back to the world I'd come to know and understand. The city life. But as parents often do, I tamped down my uncertainty and stayed the course. I stood there with a tight smile.

Lara got into the family minivan, turned around, and drove away. A trail of dust rose from her tires, and I watched until I couldn't see her anymore.

That was it. We were committed.

Standing there in the hot sun, the heavy pack on my back, the ridiculous wide-brimmed floppy hat on my head (I would almost immediately ditch that stupid thing for a basic ball cap I'd brought along), I suddenly felt alone in my responsibility for what was about to happen. After all, I was the dad, and if this trip sucked, or if it got scary, or if something horrible happened to us, it was all on me. I'd brought my son out here. I'd done this.

I became flooded with concern about all the things I didn't

know. Plus all the things I didn't know I didn't know. I noted how quiet it was now that the engine of Lara's car had faded. There wasn't a breath of wind. The only sound was the rush of the Platte River fifty yards to our left.

I swallowed my nervousness and said, "Gonna use that restroom, buddy. Might be the last one we see for a while."

"Okay." He was fiddling with the straps of his pack. I got the sense he felt a similar apprehension.

I did my business quickly. Very quickly. I didn't touch anything in that vile little concrete slime box. The freakin' thing looked like the bathroom in *Trainspotting*. I won't gross you out with a detailed description.

I returned to where Dash stood, and he was ready to go. I shouldered my pack, cinched down the shoulder straps and the thick belt, and we headed for the river.

My nervousness lingered as our boots thumped over the planks of the bridge, but I'd adventured quite a bit in my twenties, so I know it's best to just get to it. There are always worries, and it's harder for them to stick to you if you keep moving. I wanted to get down the road, I wanted to get on with it.

But…

I stopped.

Dash stopped with me. "What?"

I'd reviewed the Trail Guide in the car when we'd settled on starting with Segment 2 instead of Segment 1. The book said this was a particularly dry segment.

At this point, I should provide some background on the Colorado Trail Guide and the Colorado Trail Data Book and their differences. The Data Book is meant to be taken on the trail. It's compact, light—weighing only a few ounces—and its pages are made of a plastic-like paper, completely waterproof. But the only reason the Data Book can cover the entire trail and remain so small is because all the information has been reduced to little symbols with a legend at the beginning to tell you what those symbols mean. It shows elevation and mileage. It shows camping spots and forks in the trail. And most importantly, it tells you about water sources and how reliable they are. In short, it tells you everything you need to know to survive.

Well, in my rush to finish up my projects and get out the door, I hadn't taken the time to memorize the symbols. I didn't know how to read the Data Book. I just knew it was important, so I'd brought it along. I figured I'd have enough time to suss it out the first night we spent on the trail.

Heh. This was the beginning of my many mistakes, though I didn't know it at the time.

As a counterpoint to the Data Book, the full-blown Colorado Trail 9th Edition Trail Guide is written in plain English, with beautiful passages describing the terrain and the key spots to visit. This book is meant for pre-trail research. It's to get you in the mood to hike with anecdotal descriptions of notable spots. It also includes all the information that's in the Data Book, but the Trail Guide wasn't meant to take on the actual trail because it weighs a pound and a half.

A pound and a half. Doesn't sound like much, right? I mean, it's a book, for cryin' out loud.

It didn't sound like much to me, either, so I stuck it in my pack and brought it along. But as my ankles, knees, and back would eventually inform me, a pound and a half makes a big difference over four hundred and fifty miles. Hikers think of packable items in terms of *ounces*, not pounds. Later on the trail, I'd hem and haw about whether I ought to carry an item if it was more than a couple of ounces. If something was multiple *pounds*, there was no way I'd take it. I wouldn't even consider it unless I absolutely had to.

But I wasn't an experienced long-distance hiker that day beside the Platte River, and I was going to have to learn a few things the hard way.

I confess I'm bull-headed when it comes to learning. There are reasons for this. And there are upsides and downsides. But in short, I must make up my own mind. To me, experiencing something first-hand and listening to someone say, "You ought to do this," is not the same thing at all. I can't take another's word as gospel just because they say they are an expert.

Don't get me wrong. I do listen to and record information offered by those who have run the road before me. There's so much to learn out there in the world, and so many teachers. You should hear me excitedly yammer about Jessica Brody's *Save the Cat Writes a Novel* or Stephen King's masterful advice about prose or Craig Martelle's insight on the business side of writing. But I don't trust someone simply because they say they are an expert. I have to feel it. That's what it takes for me to become a believer. Until that moment, it's just words and possibilities, not certainties.

In addition, my fourteen-year-old self—the one who had looked out over the Animas River and thought about death—had been indelibly imprinted with this "leap before you look" sense of exploration. My I'm-scared-to-death-so-I've-just-got-to-jump form of courage had carried me through every major endeavor I'd ever attempted. And with each success, it made me more receptive to the world. It formed an attitude that had taken me to miraculous places, opened connections to amazing people, and pushed me through my most frightening moments.

It had also birthed a mysterious kind of luck I would never have dreamed possible.

Ever heard that famous quote by Goethe? *Be bold and mighty forces will come to your aid.* I'd felt those forces first-hand. I believed in them.

And I wanted Dash to believe too. I wanted to show him the world wasn't as scary as mainstream news or social media would have us believe. There isn't a psychopath waiting behind every corner to kill you. The world's default setting is to help, not hurt.

While I'd done my basic research beforehand, my default setting was to get moving and experience the details as I went. To trust, be open to the world, and to be resilient when things went in an unexpected direction. So I'd stuffed both the Trail Guide and the Data Book into my pack, intending to study up as needed on the trail.

And there, at the trailhead, ready to begin the journey with the sun shining overhead, I did what I was wired to do. I stopped by the river, pulled out the bulky Trail Guide and happily refreshed what I'd read in the car. Yep. Once we left the Platte River, this stretch of trail went ten miles with no water source.

Dash and I both had two liters of water. On flat ground in the city, I wouldn't have thought twice about that distance with that much water. No problem. But a whisper of caution stopped me. This wasn't the city. It wasn't flat ground, nor paved. And I had fifty pounds on my back.

"Hey," I said. "Maybe we should fill up the drom just in case." A drom is a lightweight, easily-foldable plastic bladder that can hold multiple gallons of water. In our case, we had a three-gallon drom to see us through some of the more water-bereft sections of the trail.

"Why?" Dash asked.

"It'd be a good time to get into the habit of using the filter," I said. "And who knows? Maybe we'll need the extra along the way. We could probably make it without, but what if I'm wrong?"

That got his attention.

"Yeah, let's filter some water," he said.

So we skitched down the embankment, set up the Platypus gravity water filter and started filling the drom. At first, I was antsy, impatient. We'd barely gone fifty feet on our journey, and the first thing we'd done was stop. It made the space between my shoulder blades itch. I wanted to get on with it. I wanted to prove we could actually do this!

Instead, I tried to relax by getting into the process.

Originally, I hadn't intended to use a gravity water filter. I had intended to use Aqua Mira, which is the latest replacement for the ages-old, tried-and-true iodine pill. You fill up a cup of water, drop in a pill, and wait a few minutes. *Voila*, drinkable water.

Iodine has been used to purify water for decades. It kills all the bad stuff: bacteria, viruses, fungi, protozoa—even the spores of bacteria and fungi. But it tastes yucky.

Aqua Mira does the same thing as iodine but without the iodine. Instead, it creates a germicidal agent by releasing a nascent form of oxygen, which activates the moment it touches water and blows up those little nasties. And apparently the water tastes just fine after. It's only oxygen, after all.

Does the Aqua Mira water actually taste good in real life? I actually don't know. I never used the tablets because, at the last minute, I purchased the Platypus gravity water filter, and the Aqua Mira tablets became my backup.

But as I stood before the fast-flowing, probably-filled-with-bacteria-and-protozoa Platte River, I hesitated. I knew what the experts said; now I needed to see for myself.

I'd tested the thing back at home, but only to make sure that water would flow from the dirty bag, through the tube and the filter, into the clean bag. And I'd used tap water. I hadn't gone out into the back yard where squirrels had danced through a mud puddle and filtered that. All I really knew was that the mechanics worked.

So I got a little nervous as I set up the filter. I began to wonder how any mere filtration system could match swords with the tried-and-true iodine, but the Platypus gravity filter had been recommended to me by my friend Chris Mandeville's son. He had hoped to hike the CT this year but couldn't string the necessary days together around his job, and he'd sworn up and down that I wanted to take a gravity filter.

I dipped the dirty bag into the moving stream and swept it out, full of brownish water that swirled with little particles. Oh boy.

I hung up the dirty bag, and gravity pulled the water through the tubes, through the filter, and into the clean bag. I held it up to the light and scrutinized it. Sure enough, it had zero particles in it. But would I really be able to see protozoa with the naked eye? I didn't think so. I saluted Dash with a smile anyway and took a drink of the newly filtered water.

And I set my internal clock to expect dysentery in a few hours.

I didn't know it at the time, but Chris's son was right. That

Platypus was the single most important piece of equipment we'd use, except, perhaps, for our shoes. Yes, it did work. And it never once failed us. Every significant memory I have of the trip includes a glimpse of that water filter in the background with its two-bag system, rubber tubes, and filter cylinder.

But at that moment, drinking that water was an act of faith.

We packed everything up, including the swollen drom of extra water, and got underway again. Finally.

The trail led us up and away from the Platte, and the thickly clustered pine trees thinned out. We hiked past dry-looking sandstone and several great swaths that had burned sometime in the past.

"How long since the fire, do you think?" Dash asked.

"I don't know," I said. I'm sure that a tree expert could have looked at that burned forest and known, but I didn't know much about trees. For all I knew, a burned tree in this high desert and low humidity could stay preserved for a hundred years.

The bright sun combined with the blackened tree trunks made me feel hotter than I probably actually was. I took a cooling swallow of water, glad we'd decided to take along the extra. Better safe than sorry.

We saw several people day-hiking over the course of the first three miles. Apparently we weren't as far from civilization as I'd thought. The first part of this trail was well-used.

But after those first few miles, the traffic fell off, and we were all alone as far as we could see in either direction. I settled into the rhythm of just walking in the beautiful sun in a place that most people don't go. When I tired of that, I pulled out the giant Trail Guide and thumbed through it, looking to make sure we were staying on course.

I was paranoid there would be a thousand different paths branching off that could fool an unwary hiker. I searched for landmarks on those pages, looked for descriptions that I matched to the land we marched through.

But I soon realized there weren't a thousand trails

branching off from the CT. In fact, in most places it's impossible to get lost. There's only one trail, and it cuts through the wilderness like a giant arrow pointing, "This way!"

There are only certain places where a hiker has to pay close attention, most notably when there's a fork in the road in the middle of nowhere. Sometimes there aren't signs, or the signs are small, and a hiker occupied with their own thoughts could step right past the fork and hike for miles in the wrong direction. Dash and I would make that mistake a couple of times. Once to the tune of about two miles of added distance. Ugh.

In short: I was on edge that first day. There was supposed to be an old quartz mine within the first mile of the hike, and I had no idea if we'd passed it or not.

I began doing an experiment: calculating our mileage so I could make a decent guess as to where we were on the trail. If I wasn't so ridiculously lame in getting around to understanding the Data Book, I would have realized that determining one's mileage was easy. Instead, I used the giant Trail Book and didn't look at the charts and symbols, but rather at the text. It told a story, and *that* I could understand.

The Data Book remained unused, stuffed into the top pouch of my pack.

Instead, I calculated our mileage based on time, which was a fun game—if a deeply flawed way to determine distance. I set the timer on my phone at a landmark I was relatively sure of, then let it run until we reached another landmark I was relatively sure of (sometimes as much as three miles away), then worked out our approximate minutes per mile. I'd then reverse that, set the timer again, and when we hit that minutes-per-mile mark, I'd call out to Dash, "We've gone another mile!" or "We should be two miles from the next landmark!"

So scientific…

We often wouldn't reach a landmark as soon as I'd anticipated. Or sometimes we'd blow right by the landmark and not realize it until much later.

But it made us feel like we were getting somewhere, and

we tinkered around with our speed. If I remember correctly, we averaged twenty-two-minute miles that first day. That's roughly three miles per hour.

Our first surprise on the trail—aside from the fact that we were drinking way more water than I'd anticipated (yay for filling the drom!)—was when we were hiking amidst light trees and sandstone slopes, rounded a bend in the path, and came across our first Colorado Trail long-distance hiker.

She had set up her one-person tent no more than six feet from the trail. She looked up and smiled. It was still early afternoon, but she had her stove out and was in the process of cooking dinner.

"Hi," I greeted her.

"Hi." She grinned. "Great day, yes?"

"Indeed," I said. "Your campsite looks cozy."

"Thanks," she said. "It looked like a good spot."

"I'm Todd, and this is my son Dash."

"I'm Prov," she said.

It sounded like a strange name, and I wondered where she was from. Did I detect a European accent?

She must have caught the confusion on my face, because she said, "It's my trail name."

"What's a trail name?" I asked.

"Is this your first thru-hike?" she asked.

What's a thru-hike? I thought. But I didn't want to seem like a complete novice right out of the gate, so I didn't ask that one. "Well, I hiked when I was a kid," I said. "Did a five-day hike once, but this is our first time on The Colorado Trail. And it's Dash's first big hike ever."

"What a great thing to do with your son," she said. Then, to Dash, "How old are you?"

"Fourteen," he said.

"That's wonderful," she said. "So a trail name is something someone on the trail gives to you. You can't make it up for yourself. And it almost always has something to do with what you've done on the trail. I got mine when I hiked the AT and carried too much of everything. Too much water. Too much food. Too many items from my home life that I didn't need. I was constantly giving things away to make my pack lighter. I *provided* whatever any other hiker needed. Provider. Prov."

"Outstanding," I said, liking this notion of trail names. I'm a sucker for nicknames. As far back as college, I'd always made up nicknames for my friends. When Lara and I chose names for our children, I leaned toward choices that would allow the kids to have good nicknames.

"Well, you don't seem like you carry too much anymore," I continued. There was nothing non-essential in her set-up.

"No, not anymore. I learned my lesson. I probably lean the other direction now. My kit is pretty sparse. But weight-wise, water is the real killer. Most people carry way too much. It's really heavy."

"Oh?" I said, thinking of the two gallons in the drom on my back. Do you know how much two gallons of water weighs? It's about seventeen pounds. That's the same as eleven Trail Guides. Yeesh!

I wondered if I shouldn't be carrying so much water.

"So you mentioned thru-hiking," I asked Prov. "What's the difference between hiking and thru-hiking?"

"Oh," she said. "Thru-hiking means you plan to hike the whole trail. Some people day-hike. Some hike a few full segments over the weekend. But thru-hikers go start to finish at one time. Denver to Durango. I'm thru-hiking."

"Ah! Okay. Well, so are we. We're going all the way."

"Good." She smiled.

She seemed happy to continue talking, but I began to feel like we were invading her space. I mean, it was so narrow between the sandstone outcropping and her tent that we were essentially standing in her campsite. She was a captive audience unless we moved along, and I didn't want to her to feel uncomfortable.

"This was all really helpful," I said. "Thank you."

"Maybe I'll see you later on the trail," she said.

"Oh?"

"Sure. You'll pass someone, then they'll pass you, then

you'll pass them again. You'll see."

"Really?"

"Unless they're northbounders. Then you'll only see them once."

I had to chuckle because she had used another unfamiliar term, but I could piece that one together. Northbounder. Going Durango to Denver instead of the other way around.

We waved goodbye and, as Dash and I continued on, I thought about our interaction with Prov. She'd been so friendly it had buoyed my spirits. There had been a kind of recognition, a kinship of thru-hikers. She'd immediately treated us with respect and welcome.

This was a feeling I'd come to experience many more times.

We kept walking, eating up another six miles or so, and we finally drank the last of the water in our one-liter Vapur bottles. We found an out-of-place glade of trees, complete with a fallen log for a bench, and we broke out the drom.

"Okay, not gonna lie, this was heavy." I hauled the two-gallon bag of water out of my pack. "But I'm glad we have it."

Dash nodded and we refilled our Vapurs. We also snacked on blueberry crisp Clif Bars. As we sat there, another hiker approached. At first I thought it was Prov, but then I realized this woman was smaller and had brown hair. She was in her mid-twenties, I'd guess, and she was moving fast.

"Hi," I greeted her as she approached.

"Hi," she replied, a little out of breath.

"Warm out, yeah?" I said.

"More than I thought," she said, slowing as she neared. "Trying to make it to the fire station."

According to the Trail Guide, Segment 2 ended at a highway where there was a volunteer fire station with a water spigot.

"I think it's about two miles away," I said.

"Yeah. Just used the last of my water," she said.

"Hey," I said. "We've got extra, if you want some."

She paused as she drew alongside us, as though thinking it

over, then shook her head. "That's nice. But no thank you. I can make it." And off she went.

The woman's urgency infected us both, and we finished our snack quickly. It was late afternoon and I wasn't positive just how far ahead the end of the segment was. I honestly didn't know anything. I was still a little skeptical that I could rely on the Trail Guide. What if there was no water? What if there was no campsite? I didn't want to have to figure out the solutions to such problems in the dark.

We powered through, heading up and over a gentle ridge. The wooded boulder clusters gave way to a wide, rocky desert expanse. The burn we'd seen earlier was in evidence here, too. It looked like there had never been many trees in the first place, but the few that had been here had been crisped. Sage brush and squarish rock outcroppings dotted the landscape, and it was hot.

We set ourselves to trying to keep up with the woman who'd passed us, but it soon became clear that, no matter how fast we hiked, we weren't going to catch her.

"She's fast," Dash said.

"Fleet," I agreed. Already I was slower than I'd assumed, and I was the one setting the pace. Dash was pretty much just following me.

But I reassured myself: it was the first day, and we'd gain speed as our legs got conditioned.

However…I had gotten a few hot spots on my feet, places where I could feel friction against my boots. There was one on the outside of each heel, and then one on the outside front of each foot, just behind the big toe. I barely acknowledged the discomfort and made a mental note to put some mole skin on those spots tonight.

Then, seemingly out of nowhere, the skies clouded up to the west. It was still bright blue directly overhead, with the sun beating down, but a light rain began to fall on us. There was no lightning, no thunder. Just rain falling straight out of the blue.

"Cool!" Dash said.

The rain stopped, then came again, then stopped. We

paused to protect our packs with rain flies. I thought about putting on my raincoat and rain pants, but I was hot and, frankly, the rain felt good.

We marched on, and by the time the storm abated, we were both wet, top to bottom, shirt to shoes, although we'd kept our packs dry. We stopped for a break and a quick snack while we rolled up our rain flies and put them away.

"That felt nice," Dash said, slicking the rainwater from his forehead back into his hair.

"Totally," I agreed.

Behind him, as the clouds moved farther south and away from us, a vibrant double rainbow appeared in the sky. It shimmered into existence, then grew brighter and brighter.

"Look at that!" I alerted Dash, who was facing away.

I'd seen a double rainbow before, but nothing like this. I could discern every color in the spectrum. Hot red blending to sunset orange, then to buttery yellow and all the way through indigo and dusky violet at the bottom. It was breathtaking. The second rainbow, arcing just above the first, was faded but still brighter than most of the *single* rainbows I'd seen in my life.

"Wow," I said, snapping pictures. "Just wow."

We snacked on almonds and beef jerky, then set out again. I sloshed forward in my wet shoes, feet slipping a little bit, hitting those hot spots. I ignored them. I'd walked in wet shoes before. And my feet were going to have to toughen up anyway.

I was wearing a hitherto-unused pair of hiking boots I'd bought on Amazon eight years ago. They'd been gathering dust in my closet because they *almost* fit well, but not quite. And I'd missed the deadline for returning them. I'd been angry about that and had always wanted to force those boots to be useful.

And I had decided The Colorado Trail was the place to make them earn out their purchase price.

Every experienced hiker reading this is probably wincing right now. Because one of the cardinal rules of hiking is to get your shoes right. Happy feet, happy hike. Without your feet, you're going nowhere.

Strangely, I had made that an absolute priority for my son.

I'd been meticulous about finding the right shoes for him. We'd gone shopping and he'd tried on pair after pair until he found some trail runners that "felt perfect."

At that time, I had also tried on several pairs, even purchased some boots that I ended up returning because they really hadn't fit better than the ones I already had. So my goal? Break in the old ones. After all, that was the way we did it when I was a kid. You get new shoes, they're never quite right, and you walk in them until they are.

I'd also paid money for them which I couldn't get back, and they were just gathering dust in my closet. I was determined to *make* them work. I had seen these hiking boots as "valuable" and I just couldn't let them go.

I'm not a complete idiot. Please understand. It's just...I had scars.

You see, the aftermath of my parents' divorce had introduced me to real need and lack for the first time ever. My mother, as a newly single parent, had struggled to support us. She had three kids but only a minimum wage job slinging chicken at KFC. Our broken little family dropped from middle-class to poor pretty much within one summer. We moved out of our big four-bedroom, three-bathroom house into a two-bedroom duplex in town. My mother, realizing she couldn't afford that rental, moved us to a different rental, soon realized she couldn't afford that one, and moved us into an old, single-wide trailer fifteen miles out of town.

Turned out she couldn't afford that one, either.

That was when my young mind awoke to the low-grade terror of sinking finances. I remember lying awake on a thick blanket on the floor—she'd sold our bunk beds—listening to my mom talk in hushed tones down the hallway. The quiet desperation in her voice twisted my heart as she confided to her friend that she didn't know what to do next. She'd had to sell a piece of furniture every month just to make the trailer payment. After a few more months, we'd be out of furniture, out of money, and out of a place to live.

I'll never forget that cold, paralyzing feeling. Since that

day, I'd made the absolute most out of all of my possessions, from tools to cars to portable stereos to clothes. I mean, I can get dandied up if I need to. I've had jobs that required it, and I've worn tuxes and slick shoes at many an event. I've worn thin, svelte gloves, overcoats, neckties, and suits. But leave me to my own devices and I'll wear the same T-shirts and cargo pants until they are literally falling apart before I buy new ones. Why? Because sometimes—you never know when—resources might run out. And then you've got what you've got and you have to make the best of it.

So those boots looked and felt just fine to me as I stared at that gorgeous rainbow.

But I was headed for a reckoning.

When we rolled into camp that night, I had four blisters and no idea how big a problem it was going to become.

6

PURPLE MOUNTAINS

AT THE END OF SEGMENT 2, with the sun low in the sky, we searched for the volunteer fire station, which was the next landmark where we could get water. By this time, we'd actually gone through our spare water and needed to refill. But as we hiked up to the highway, the only visible building stood on a rise on the other side of the road, encircled by a barbed wire fence. At least three signs hung on the fence warning: "No Trespassers!"

Are we supposed to sneak in there? I thought. I'd assumed whoever had made the Trail Guide wouldn't lead us to a place where we'd have to do something illegal, but...

I fumbled with the book, opened it up.

"Is that it, Dad?" Dash looked at the signs dubiously, probably thinking the same thing I was.

It took me a long parched minute as I re-read the text and found a passage saying the fire station was a tenth of a mile up the road, and I let Dash know.

"Are you sure?" he asked.

"Let's just take a look," I said. I wasn't sure at all, actually, and I grew concerned as we headed east along Highway 550. What if that building on the rise *was* the station? What if we'd have to sneak in? We had no water, and the next source, according to the Trail Guide, was three miles away. We were already uncomfortably thirsty. I couldn't imagine making it through the night—let alone hiking three miles—without water.

Dash and I hiked for a tenth of a mile up the highway and did find the actual fire station. But after seeing all the "No Trespassing" signs on that previous building, I was edgy. I wondered just how legit this was, taking water from a spigot that clearly belonged to the fire station. I approached, imagining a confrontation with some angry fireman who was sick and tired of free-loading hikers stealing water.

We reached the building with its four two-story garage doors, behind which, no doubt, lay the fire trucks. Next to them, a human-sized door opened, and a fireman came out. He spotted us and turned our direction.

I swallowed.

"Looking for the water?" he asked.

"Uh, yeah," I said.

"'Round to the side." He poked a thumb over his shoulder. "Got a few others back there too. Can't miss it. Hot day, yeah?"

"Yeah," I said, relaxing. "Thank you. Thank you so much."

Dash immediately headed in the direction of the indicated spigot.

"Pretty cool thing you're doing, hiking the trail," the fireman said.

"Pretty cool thing you're doing, letting us use your water," I responded.

"Ah." He waved it away. "We like to support you guys. That your son?" he asked, nodding at Dash's back.

"It is indeed," I said.

"That must be nice."

"I'm not gonna lie. It's pretty freakin' cool," I said.

He smiled. "Well, you look thirsty. Take as much as you want."

"Thanks again."

I rounded the corner of the building to find Dash talking with two other hikers—a college-age man and the fleet-footed woman who'd blazed past us on the trail.

I'm crap at learning names. I usually have to ask people several times before I can memorize them, unless I specifically concentrate on retaining them the first time around by creating a mnemonic device. I was far too tired and thirsty for any of that. So when the fleet-footed woman and the other hiker told me their names, they sailed right past me as I drank and drank that cool, wonderful water.

I can't adequately describe the feeling of suddenly having as much water as we wanted after being so miserly with it. The sheer decadence of it. The refreshing taste. And I'm sure it was all accented by the fact that we hadn't been sure until this moment that we'd even be able to slake our thirst.

It took about sixty seconds to go from parched to sated. Then I was refreshed and ready to go. It's amazing how quickly the body readjusts.

The nearest campsite was close, about half a mile away, and after filling up the drom for cooking, plus the four one-liter Vapurs, we shouldered our packs once more.

"You headed to camp?" the fleet-footed woman asked.

"Uh, yeah," I said. "Just up ahead."

"Me too. Hike together?"

"Dash?" I turned to him.

"Sure," he said.

"Cool." I snapped my fingers like I was trying to remember her name—though there wasn't a chance of that—and I said, "Tell me your name again?"

"Gretchen," she said.

"Nice to meet you, Gretchen. I'm Todd and this is Dash."

"Nice to meet you."

We got our packs on and spent the next ten minutes trying to keep up with her as she set a blistering pace. I tried to imagine walking that fast all day long.

We reached the campsite, which had lots of flat ground near an old dirt road that went up to a rise in the distance. As Dash and I surveyed the site, we respectfully waited for Gretchen to choose her spot first, then dropped our gear a good hundred feet away to give her space. I wasn't sure what camping etiquette was for thru-hikers, so I wanted to err on the side of respect, rather than presumption. But I did ask her if she wanted to have dinner with us, and she agreed, joining us for our Harmony House dehydrated meal of spiced pinto beans and peppers.

Dash and I set about putting our camp up, which took us about thirty minutes. Gretchen finished her set-up in ten.

We rested. We ate. We drank as much water as we wanted, and we enjoyed the conversation with Gretchen. I told her about our home life, that I was an epic fantasy novelist, and Dash was going into high school next year. She told us she was an accountant with just a couple weeks off, and she was determined to walk a chunk of the CT during that time. She'd started today at the beginning of Segment 1 and had gone over twenty-eight miles! Dash and I were both stunned and impressed. We'd hiked eleven miles after a noon start-time and had been proud of it. She did acknowledge that twenty-eight miles was a big day for her, and that she planned to moderate her pace a bit tomorrow.

The sun set, and we began cleaning up the meal while there was still a dim light to be had. As I was washing the dishes—which consisted of walking a good distance from the campsite, dribbling water on our tin pan and cups and rubbing at them until they were rinsed out—the sunset transformed into a magical twilight—orange and purple light glowing over the rise at the end of the weed-choked dirt road. I looked up and noticed Gretchen standing atop the hill, her dark silhouette cutting into the glow.

She had to be at least a hundred yards away—possibly twice that—but her quiet voice carried to me like she was standing by my side. It was like the mountain air was so pure, sound traveled farther.

"You should come up here," she said, beckoning. I set the dishes on the tangle of dead stumps that had been my "sink" and started up the road. I crested the rise and—

My breath caught in my throat.

The rise dropped away to a valley filled with darkening purple mist. Layer upon layer of mountains rose from that mist. Foothills first, then taller mountains, then the distant mighty peaks of the Rockies. In between each layer, the mist changed color to lighter and lighter shades of purple. The valley floor was practically black, the foothills beyond them a dark purple, the next layer of mountains in indigo, and then the final, jagged row a light lavender. Those furthest peaks cut into a fading blue sky and touched the clouds, which glowed with a dull orange and yellow.

"Wow…" I said.

"Right?" she murmured, and though my gaze was fixed on the horizon, I knew she was smiling. I could hear it in her voice.

I soaked it in, then I pulled out my phone and began taking pictures. "It's only been one day," I said. "And I've already seen so many amazing things."

She didn't reply. I'd quickly come to find that Gretchen was a woman of few words.

"I have to tell Dash," I said.

She nodded.

"You mind if I call him?" I didn't want to ruin the moment by being too loud.

"Not at all."

I yelled for Dash to come see it, and he ran up the slope to enjoy the spectacle. He was just as captured by it as the two of us, and as those enchanting colors slowly faded, he turned to me.

"We're going over that, aren't we?" he said. "All those mountains."

"Yes, we are," I said softly.

"Wow."

Gretchen glanced over, a small smile on her face.

Those gorgeous colors didn't last long, and I was so happy I'd snapped some pictures. But as we walked back to camp, I flipped through my pictures to cement the moment in my mind…and was sorely disappointed. The pictures seemed drab, absolutely failing to capture the majesty of what we'd just witnessed.

But then…of course they didn't. They couldn't. Just looking at a picture of that kind of sunset—even if the photographer had been a professional—couldn't possibly deliver the same effect. Nothing could replicate that I'd been standing there, the cool air on my skin as the temperature dropped, that I'd seen the entire range of shifting colors along that horizon with my own eyes, that I'd felt the warmth of Gretchen's unexpected companionship, knowing I'd have missed all this if she hadn't called out to me.

I put my phone away and, rather than being frustrated I'd been blocked from carrying away a trophy, I felt a satisfied glow. I gingerly removed my Crocs from my tender feet and set them beneath the tent's rainfly.

"You getting any hot spots on your feet, Dash? Any blisters?" I asked for the third time that day. I'd been meticulous about a few things regarding Dash. First was to make sure he didn't fall too far behind me—I was terrified of getting separated from him. Second was to make sure he was drinking enough water. Third was to remind him to reapply sunscreen every couple of hours. A sunburn early on could ruin the whole trip for him. And the fourth was to check on his feet. While me getting blisters wasn't great, it would be twice as bad if he did. That could end the whole trip right now.

"No blisters, Dad," he said.

"Shoes fit okay?"

"Shoes are perfect, Dad."

"Good," I said. "That's good."

We zipped into the tent, tucked into our sleeping bags, and I let the whole experience linger as long as it could.

This was our first day. Just the first.

My impressions? Amazing. I was stunned by how many sights we'd seen and experiences we'd had.

We'd laughed and hiked through unforgettable canyons of sandstone and forest burn. We'd turned smiling faces heavenward as rain poured from a sunny sky. We'd stared in awe at the most colorful double rainbow I'd ever seen. We'd met interesting strangers who had welcomed us because we were fellow thru-hikers. And to top off the day, we'd witnessed that gorgeous sunset…

I already felt like a father who'd delivered an experience to his son that would serve him the rest of his life. I was doing Right with a capital "R." That was my impression of the first day.

My impression of the first night? It was hell.

7

THE FIRST NIGHT

As Dash dropped off to sleep, a smattering of city fears chipped away at my satisfaction. We were beside a dirt road. We were a quarter mile from a highway. Anyone could come along. What if someone wanted to hurt us? I mean, a tent does a great job of creating the illusion of a secure space—our own little hobbit hole—but let's face it, it's paper-thin fabric stretched over a pair of aluminum poles. It's meant to fend off the rain and create a small barrier between you and the cold. But it is absolutely no barrier to another creature. A bear could tear it open with one swipe. So could a knife.

My first leap of faith had been trusting the Platypus, then the Trail Guide. Now it was this. Sleeping in the middle of nowhere.

I was supposed to lie down, fall asleep, and assume we'd be safe. I didn't believe it, but somehow I was just supposed to.

I mean, I'm the dad. The protector. I don't get to be afraid.

But fears are fears. And here in the middle of nowhere, my

imagination had plenty of room to run.

At that point, a calming thought came to me. Gretchen was a hundred feet away. Silly, right? I was the eldest adult here. *I* should be looking out for *her*, if anything. In addition, I'm a big guy and I know how to fight. If it came down to some kind of confrontation, I'd give myself good odds against another person.

It felt illogical, but just having someone close by—knowing that if I called for help there'd be someone to hear me—was enough for me to feel safe on some instinctual level. I suddenly suspected that was why Gretchen wanted to camp near us, too.

With this patch of tranquility, I finally drifted off to sleep.

Which was when Dash began to snore.

Now, when I say Dash began to snore, we're not talking a cute little snuffling like a bunny. We're not even talking that Hollywood snore we've seen a million times, *Honk! Rumblerumblerumble…Honk! Rumblerumblerumble…*

No. This was a chainsaw trying to cut rock. It roared to life, almost making me sit bolt upright.

It's the kind of snore that, if you heard it while you were awake, you'd laugh. You'd have to laugh, because it was so ridiculous it couldn't possibly be real.

But when you've just hiked eleven miles, filled your belly with food, and desperately wanted to sleep before an even larger day tomorrow, it doesn't make you want to laugh. It makes you want to cry.

The snore abruptly stopped, leaving my nerves jangling, but the sweet silence only lent power to the sudden, stone-chipping, grinding resurgence.

It was like the chainsaw wielder had only shifted his feet to get a different angle before slamming the spinning blades back into the rock.

I laid there, eyes wide, for three hours, using mental conditioning to convince myself the snoring was okay, that it was just…a part of the world now. This, combined with extreme exhaustion, allowed me to doze fitfully.

Which was when another trio of hikers showed up late to the campsite.

It sounded like they had plunked their tent down right beside ours, and they proceeded to talk—loudly—about drinkin', huntin', how all the damned liberals ought to be shot, and their love of the movie *The Matrix*. Over the next two hours as they continued drinking and boasting, I was sure they'd get so drunk they'd start messing with the other campers nearby, dragging us out of our tents and demanding to know if we were damned liberals.

I moved the bear mace from the bottom of the tent to the top, within easy reach.

It was almost two in the morning when these drunk fellows—whose love of *The Matrix* was the only thing we seemed to have in common—finally fell asleep.

I lay awake for long minutes after they went silent before pure exhaustion dragged me down into a dreamless sleep.

It felt like I'd barely blinked before the sun lit the sides of our tent.

Oh this sucks, I thought. *This sucks so hard.*

But we had to get up and start hiking if we were going to stay on schedule. I didn't have time to lie here until I was rested. Sometimes you just have to buck up and do the job while you're exhausted.

My bones felt old and creaky as I forced myself to sit up. I told myself to make some oatmeal, get everything ready for breakfast, and then I'd feel better. Dash was still snoring away, and I decided to let him sleep. At least one of us ought to get some rest.

As I slipped on my Crocs, I felt every blister on my feet, and one of them had popped. A new present for the morning. Although the pain did help wake me up.

When I emerged from the tent, Gretchen was up, and she'd already struck camp. There was nothing left but her pack and a stretch of flat dirt where her tent had been.

"Morning," I said quietly, eyeing the tent of the Matrix-lovers, astonished to find that it was more than a hundred feet away. I could barely believe it.

"Hi," she said. "You sleep okay?"

I just chuckled ruefully. "I'm sure it'll get better once I get moving."

She gave a little smile. There was no way she hadn't heard the Matrix-lovers last night, drinking and talking up a storm. I wanted to march over there and start kicking their tent, banging pots. That would be satisfying.

My imagination took it a step further...

BREAKING NEWS: FIFTY-YEAR-OLD DIES AFTER KICKING TENT OF LOCAL BOYS

When interviewed, one of the boys had this to say:
"Well, we just thought he was one o' them robot squid-things. Or maybe a liberal. We just started shootin' 'til we was outta bullets. Didn't even open the tent."

Yeah. Maybe that was a bad idea.

"You heading out?" I asked Gretchen.

"Soon, yeah."

"Want some breakfast?"

"Gonna eat on the trail," she said. "I want to get moving."

I felt ridiculously slow. I still had to boil water, make oatmeal, eat, and pack everything up.

"I hear that," I said. "But I gotta make breakfast for the boy and treat my feet before we get moving."

"Ouch. Blisters?"

"Yeah."

"You tried duct tape?" she asked.

A sudden memory came to me. My friend Lawdon, the one I mentioned has hiked the Appalachian Trail, had actually taken time out of his schedule to come over to my house with a bunch of hiker advice the week before we left.

"Take duct tape," he'd said.

"A roll of duct tape?" I'd asked.

"Not the whole roll, dingus. Take a stick and wrap some duct tape around it. Lightweight, packable. And when you get a hot spot on your foot, cover it with duct tape. That'll at least double the toughness of your skin and take some of the friction. Might stop a blister."

That memory flashed through my head.

"Uh, I forgot to bring duct tape," I said lamely to Gretchen.

"Here." She brought up her hiking pole and there, wrapped around it just below the grip, was duct tape.

"Hey," I said. "Right on your pole. Smart."

She didn't say anything, just unwound a good amount, tore it off and handed it to me. I took Lawdon's advice and wound the strip around a thin stick.

"Thanks so much," I said.

"Of course," she said. "Thanks for dinner."

"My pleasure."

"Well." She hoisted her pack onto her shoulders. "See you on the trail."

"Sure," I said. *No way,* I thought. *Once you get going, we'll never keep up. Twenty-eight miles in a day!*

She started up the dirt road that ran by our campsite. According to the book, that road connected with the trailhead a quarter mile to the west, which was where we'd be heading shortly.

8

UNDERWEAR

AFTER SOME HOT QUAKER OATMEAL—maple and brown sugar for me, bananas & cream for Dash—I felt ready to tackle the day. Dash and I broke down the tent, stuffed our sleeping bags in their sacks, packed up our packs, and got under way. It took us about an hour.

My sleep deprivation made me slow in the head, but I'd been sleep-deprived before. Besides, I would soon discover that most of what was required of me on the trail didn't require much brainpower. Just leg power. Seventy percent of hiking is just soaking in the scenery and keeping the feet moving.

As we hiked, I found a lot of my worries drifting away, city concerns that just didn't apply here. I had no access to anything from that world. I had no chores to do, or to feel guilty about *not* doing. There were no interruptions from a beeping cell phone, no never-ending landscape of entertainment distractions at the touch of a TV remote or computer keyboard. I was free to focus on the here and now, which included nothing but me, Dash, the trees, rocks, trail, and the blue, blue sky.

After our adventure, the question others most often asked me was: "What's the main difference between home and the trail?"

Looking back, it was on Day 2 that I unwittingly began formulating the answer to this question, and it was this...

At home, I had to pay attention to four hundred and eighty-four things that were constantly nattering to get my attention: Is Dash up and getting ready for school? Why did Elowyn just scream in the middle of doing her homework? Dammit, the dog got into the trash again. Lara is rushing to get out the door and needs me to move my car. Today is trash pick-up day. It's already nine o'clock, and I didn't get my word count in yet. The cat puked on the counter. Do we have enough money in the checking account to pay the credit card bill? Do I teach taekwondo tonight? What the hell day is it?

You get my point.

The four hundred and eighty-four things that assail me in the city all seem life-threatening at the time. Is Dash going to get an "F" in Algebra? Adrenaline spike. Am I late paying the credit card bill? Adrenaline spike. Am I going to be late for my taekwondo class and keep the students waiting outside the door? Adrenaline spike. Adrenaline spike. Adrenaline spike.

But the truth is: none of these things can actually kill me. The urgency is self-created. Probably the only thing that threatens my life with regularity is driving on I-25. And the irony is: I never worry about driving. Go figure.

What's the difference between that and a trail mentality? Easy. On the trail, I only had to pay attention to seven essential things:

1. Water
2. Food
3. Footing near cliffs
4. The weather
5. Wild animals
6. Adequate clothing
7. Shelter at night

And I had to make sure Dash paid attention to them as well. If we dropped our focus on any of those seven items—with the possible exception of number seven—it could kill us. Honest-to-God, dead-as-a-doornail kill us.

Inadequate clothing? Hypothermia. Get between a moose and his lake? Hoof-shaped holes in your chest. Don't pay attention and step off a cliff? Splat. Not enough food or water? Duh.

The only thing on the list that wasn't unequivocally life threatening, but that I paid attention to anyway, was shelter. I mean, it could certainly lead to hypothermia if you couldn't get out of the elements, but we met a few hikers who didn't carry a tent. They "cowboy camped" and slept right on the ground underneath the stars.

But the rest of it? Legitimately essential to preserving life and limb.

We hiked on, I kept an easy eye on my seven essentials, and my fatigue settled into serenity. I felt like I'd blended into my surroundings. Everything I could be doing, I *was* doing, and my mind eased, freeing up all my energy to pour into my legs. And better yet, the duct tape seemed to be helping with my blisters. Bonus.

As we began a long, steep incline, Dash struggled for the first time. As the trail went up and up and up, he began to lag while I ranged out ahead. The first time I lost sight of him, I waited for him to catch up and we implemented a whistle system to keep track of each other. If I got too far ahead, I'd whistle. If he whistled back, I'd assume everything was fine and I'd keep going. If I didn't hear him whistle at all, I'd assume he hadn't heard me and I'd wait for him.

We made it up that climb and onto a ridge that came to a nearly three-hundred-and-sixty-degree vista. The promontory had flat ground for camping, and someone had built a fire ring between a series of boulder clusters.

"Cool campsite," I said, wishing it was late enough in the day to justify plunking down here for the night. "This would be a great place to stay."

"Yeah," Dash said. He popped the catch on his belt, dropped his pack, and began climbing the boulders. I looked at the purple mountains in the distance, set against the blue sky. This was why we'd come here. Nothing out here but us, the fresh air, the wilderness…

And a pair of boxer briefs.

I laughed. After all of my highfalutin thoughts about the purity of nature, it was like the Universe was poking fun at me. There in front of the fire ring was a neglected pair of black boxer briefs.

"Somebody walked off without their underwear," I said as Dash jumped down off a boulder.

"Ew," he said.

I whipped out my phone.

"What are you doing?" Dash demanded.

"Taking a picture."

"Gross!"

"Are you kidding? We've got this gorgeous vista, breathtaking pure mountain wilderness. We're all alone in the middle of nowhere. Except, uh oh! No, we aren't. There's a freakin' pair of underwear. Aren't you curious about its story? Why is it here? How could someone just walk off without their underwear? Is it some joking message from one hiker to another? Or did they leave it to mess with strangers like us? Or did they just not realize their underwear had fallen off, and they started hiking without it?"

"I'm leaving." Dash shouldered his pack, clicked the belt on, and started down the trail.

"This is real-life irony, in the middle of nowhere!" I called after him.

"You're gross," he said over his shoulder.

I chuckled and followed him.

The clusters of tumbledown boulders continued and, once we were long past the underwear grossness, Dash proclaimed this part of the trail as his favorite so far.

It was the first time he'd claimed a favorite spot, but it wasn't to be the last. There were twenty-eight segments of the

Colorado Trail, and Dash would proclaim his favorite part half a dozen times in the coming days.

9
FOOD FROM THE HEAVENS

OVER THE COURSE OF THE TWELVE MILES of Segment 3, my hopes for the duct tape were dashed. It only lasted an hour before slipping off. I tried re-taping my feet, but the tape slipped off even faster once I'd been walking a while. Sweat was a problem. Duct tape doesn't stick to sweat. Lawdon had mentioned the duct tape fix was good for hot spots, *before* blisters really came on, and I wondered if I'd sailed past that moment. I winced and bore the blisters, expecting I'd just have to push through until they started getting better.

"Dash, how are your feet?" I called ahead.

"Could you stop talking about your feet?" he called back.

"I'm not talking about my feet. I'm talking about *your* feet."

"I think you're still kinda talking about *your* feet."

I laughed. "Okay, I'll stop talking about everybody's feet if you'll just answer the q uestion."

"Feet are fine, Dad," he called back. "Shoes are great."

"Okay okay…" I chuckled.

We hiked through terrain with boulders and intermittent

forests, covering a good twelve miles before setting up camp that night. We didn't have any Matrix-lovers joining us, but Dash's snoring reigned supreme. I struggled to get sleep, tossing and turning, drifting into dreams only to get yanked out again.

But when the sun rose, I got up and got my body moving again. If we were to keep to our schedule, we had to average fifteen miles a day, and we hadn't had a single fifteen-miler yet.

Day three brought beautiful, green-wooded areas. No burn or pine beetle devastation. We wound through the fresh-smelling forest with the trail turning this way and that. The ground was mostly flat—no big climbs like yesterday—and Dash seemed to be settling happily into a groove. He even ranged out in front of me from time to time as I babied my feet.

Every hour of hiking took us further away from any roads, and I began to feel a kind of coziness in the woods. I was even getting used to the constant temperature changes. The higher we went, the more the temperature vacillated, hot and cold by turns. We'd head across an open field, and I'd start to sweat. Layers came off. We'd head into shadowy woods, and I'd start to shiver. Layers went back on.

Putting on and taking off my long-sleeved tech shirt three or four times in an hour wasn't unusual.

Of course, no matter whether Dash was wearing a T-shirt, a T-shirt-plus-fleece, or T-shirt-fleece-rain-jacket combo, he wore nothing but shorts on his legs. It was like they were invulnerable to cold.

At about three o'clock we rounded a corner, came out of the woods, and started up a gentle rise. Based on what I could decipher of the Trail Guide, the next campsite was five and a half miles down the path, which was about perfect. Our pace was a solid three miles per hour, and the sun went down around five-thirty. So if we pushed, we would not only make our fifteen-mile goal, but we'd get our tent set up before dark.

We came over the rise and descended into the most striking valley I'd ever seen. The North Fork Lost Creek ran right down the middle of it, and everything was green.

"Wow," I murmured to Dash.

"This is my favorite part," he said for the second time. "We have to take Mom here."

"She would love this," I said.

But by the time we reached the creek, leaden clouds hung low in the skies. I couldn't see a scrap of blue anywhere. The trail forked just as it reached the water, and the left-hand path led over a bridge to the most picturesque campsite we'd seen. Wide swaths of cute, flat campgrounds nestled underneath the protective boughs of tall pine trees. It would not only give protection from the sun, but a little from the rain, too. And, of course, there was a plentiful water source.

We both paused.

"That looks great," Dash said.

We were still more than five miles from our planned campsite. If we were going to hit that fifteen-mile mark, we had to keep moving.

"You want to stay here, buddy? Or do you want to try and make fifteen?" I asked.

"No. Let's keep going." He didn't even hesitate. "When we take Mom here, that's where we'll camp."

"Agreed."

We continued on, paralleling the creek, and a light rain began. It persisted for more than five minutes, so we put on our rain gear.

We hiked fast alongside the creek, the forests on either side set back about a hundred feet from the water.

"I bet the trail tucks back into the forest up ahead," I said. "And we'll be able to get out of the rain somewhat."

"The book says that?" Dash asked.

"No, I'm just reading the lay of the land. I don't think the trail makers would have the trail going alongside the creek for long. It'll probably cross in about a mile or so, then we'll head into that forest." I pointed.

I'd later look back on this moment and roll my eyes. I had no basis for my assurance. I just wanted to believe it. It fit my plan nicely. In reality, I didn't know what the hell I was talking about.

But I was the father. I was in charge. Therefore, I was supposed to know what I was talking about. And in my city life, acting like one knows what one is talking about actually works. Fake it till you make it, right? There are very real benefits to projecting confidence. Strangely, it often gets things done.

But Mother Nature isn't swayed by confidence, and she doesn't give a shit what you think you know.

After thirty minutes of hiking, the trail continued alongside the creek, and the rain worsened. Our packs and our upper bodies were dry, but from the waist down we were soaked.

Then the first lightning boomed in the distance.

Dash stopped and peered back at me beneath the shadow of his hood. "Dad?" he said.

"Yeah," I said. "Not a great idea to be out in the open in a lightning storm." That much, I *did* know.

"That's what I was thinking," he said.

On top of everything else, my blistered feet were beginning to sting. I badly wanted to get to the next campsite and take a look at them. My whole macho thing was wearing thin, and my feet were not "toughening up" fast enough. It had started to penetrate my thick skull that walking in the rain and not drying my feet out was probably a big mistake. Continuing to hike in the rain for several more miles seemed like the last thing I should do.

The addition of the lightning was the final straw. It pulled me up short, made me question my decision to press on. I really wanted to get to the next campsite, but hiking in a lightning storm was a bad idea.

"Let's take shelter in those trees and decide what to do," I said.

"Okay," Dash said.

We charged up the slope about a hundred feet and huddled in a stand of pine trees. The rain came so hard now that the spiny branches overhead only helped a little.

"It'll blow over soon," I said optimistically.

"Yeah," he said, and we watched the rain for another fifteen minutes.

"It's not stopping," Dash finally said. "How far are we from where the trail goes into the woods?"

"I don't know. I might be wrong about that. I've actually been meaning to get up to speed on the Data Book."

"Let me see it," he said, holding out his hand. "Seems like a good time to figure it out."

It was the first time he'd taken charge of a situation, and I loved it. This whole trip was about him learning his limits and pushing himself, and it made me warm inside to see it in action. I'd been putting off figuring out the Data Book, and he was putting an end to that right here. He was taking charge of our destiny a little bit, taking on some responsibility. It was awesome.

I opened the top of my pack, rummaged around, moving aside my remote phone charger, the first-aid kit, my money clip, business card holder, matches, paper for starting a fire, my spoon, and a Ziploc of trail mix. Then my hands closed on the pristine, never-before-used Data Book. I passed it over to him.

There in the rain by the side of the trail, Dash took the time to decipher the symbols. Turns out, it wasn't rocket science. I felt a fool for not studying it sooner.

The book got liberally dripped on, but that didn't hurt it one bit. Its plastic pages had been designed for exactly this.

With Dash's nose buried in the book, I scanned the horizon, and I caught sight of another hiker down by the creek. He didn't seem to be hurrying to get out of the rain. In fact, he was strolling and throwing a ball for his dog. Lightning flashed in the distance, and the rumble of thunder rolled closer, but it didn't seem to bother him.

"Look at that guy," I said.

Dash's cowled head rose as I pointed toward the creek. "What's he doing?" he said. "Just hanging out in the rain?"

"My point," I said.

"Why isn't he afraid of the lightning?"

"Let's go ask him."

He glanced at me.

"You stay here," I said. "I'll come back for you."

"Naw. I'll go." He slapped the wet book shut and handed it to me. I stowed it.

We shouldered our packs and headed into the rain again, hiked down to the guy. He was decked out in full rain gear, head to toe, but he had no pack.

"Hi!" I waved.

He waved back.

"You don't seem to be afraid of the lightning," I said.

He shrugged. "Not really much danger down here," he said. "The creek's the low point. And there's a lot of trees around."

Ah! That made sense to me, and my mind eased a little. "Oh. Okay. Have fun!" We hiked back to the trail.

I turned to Dash. "Well, I'm not as worried about the lightning anymore," I said. "That's a little reassuring."

"Yeah, but it's four miles to the next campsite. We wanna hike four miles in this?"

"Point. Okay, the way I see it, we've got choices. We hike another four miles in the rain. After which, we set up camp in the rain, in the dark. Or…" I looked back toward where we'd come from. "We take the loss, hike backward, settle for nine miles today and camp in that place we just left."

"Well, I'm cold," he said. "Hiking in this sucks."

"Truth."

"But I don't want to lose an hour's worth of hiking. Hiking back sucks, too."

"I feel you," I agreed.

He sighed. "Okay. Let's hike back. I guess this is a lesson. We should have camped at that awesome spot when we first reached it. Next time, if it's late, we're at a good campsite and it's raining, we stop."

"Agreed," I said. I felt a twist of disappointment that we weren't going to make our mileage today, but I felt a deeper relief that my poor feet were going to get a break in a very short half an hour.

We started back with a fervor, heads-down against the rain with such single-minded focus it barely seemed fifteen minutes before we arrived at that beautiful campsite.

The first thing I did was strip off my wet shoes and socks and dry my poor feet. I gingerly slid them into my silver Crocs, and I sent a fervent prayer of gratitude to Megan, wherever she was. She had prevailed upon me to take the Crocs as my "camp shoes."

"You're going to want camp shoes," she had said. "And Crocs are perfect. They're lightweight and comfy. My sister says camp shoes are a little bit of paradise at the end of a long day."

Boy oh boy had she been right. It was exactly like that. A little piece of paradise.

Dash and I set up the tent, then quickly donned dry clothes. And, of course, the rain cleared up only a few minutes later. It was like a sign from the Universe that we'd made the right choice.

As I hung the wet clothes on the low-hanging boughs of the pine tree and set up the stove, I limped gingerly about. My machismo was entirely gone, and now I felt a foreboding. What if I couldn't just muscle through this? What if I'd made a big mistake? This was painful. Like, really painful. I began to think about more than just the pain. If the blisters turned into open wounds, how much longer could I safely hike without doing permanent damage? Or getting an infection?

I put the thought from my mind. We were four days into the hike, a full day from any kind of civilization. There was simply no choice right now. Tomorrow morning, I'd just strap on my shoes and make the best of it.

After I finished setting up the stove, I limped off into the woods with the trowel and toilet paper to do my business and bury it. This was my least favorite part of camping. Bathrooms are an amazing cultural advance that we take for granted every single day.

When I came back to the campsite, I moved on to another

worry that had been plaguing me. I began pulling our food from the pack and laying it out in front of me. I'd allotted a certain amount for breakfast, lunch, and dinner, and I'd noticed we were eating more than what I'd planned.

Dash came up behind me. "What are you doing?" he asked.

I looked up from the lines of tuna packets, Clif Bars, peanut butter packets, trail mix, almonds and the Ziploc bags of our freeze-dried vegan dinners, each a unique concoction Elo and I had created from the Harmony House bulk supplies.

"We've got three days left to hike before our first resupply in Breckenridge," I said.

"Yeah."

"That's assuming we can hit that fifteen-mile-a-day average. And we're averaging about ten," I said.

"Yeah," he said, looking back at the pile, then back at me.

"I think I made a mistake in the planning," I said. "This might not be enough food."

He sat down next to me and started sorting it, going through the same motions I had, no doubt thinking about how much he'd eaten so far, and about how much we would need over the next three days.

I felt a warm pride watching him do the math, come to his own conclusions.

But I was pretty sure already. The first day, we'd gleefully eaten whatever we'd wanted. The second day we'd done pretty much the same. On the third day, I'd noted this, and I curbed my intake, though I hadn't stopped Dash from eating what he needed. He was fourteen, after all, and there wasn't a scrap of fat on him. He needed all he could get. Me, on the other hand, I had a bit of caloric reserve just waiting to be used.

Our planned daily intake was supposed to look like this:
- Breakfast — One packet Quaker oatmeal each.
- Lunch — One tuna packet, one Clif Bar, one packet of Justin's peanut butter each.
- Dinner — A cup full of purely vegetable-based, high-calorie Harmony House combinations. Beans and

potatoes and corn and such. Each of us was to have at least a cup every night.
- Snacks — A bag of trail mix. A few extra Clif Bars. A few extra peanut butter packets. Hot chocolate. A Ziploc of lemonade. A couple of dehydrated ice cream bars Lara had thrown in there for fun.

Dash had doubled up on oatmeal in the mornings and Clif Bars at lunch from the start. I hadn't worried about it at first because I'd packed extra, but not a specified amount of extra. Just, you know, "extra." I'd thought in terms of my city life intake, planning meals that would have satisfied me there. I hadn't tallied up the likely calorie burn. That, I was suddenly realizing, was a pretty bad oversight.

I took the time to do that now.

One packet of Quaker oatmeal ranged from a hundred thirty to a hundred and seventy calories, depending on the flavor. One tuna packet, about a hundred thirty. Clif Bar? Let's say a solid two-fifty. Justin's peanut butter? A hundred ten. And let's say our dinners gave us a thousand. They didn't, but let's say that for the sake of optimism. So…at maximum, with snacks, I'd planned for us to have an intake of about two thousand one hundred calories a day each, plus a little extra. That's just right for me on a normal day, and probably good for someone Dash's size and age. But that's city life. Maybe with a bit of exercise thrown in.

Next I calculated how much someone of my size would burn from eight hours of hiking.

It's six thousand. Conservatively.

"Shit," I said.

"What?" Dash asked.

"We don't have enough food."

The good news was that Dash had already been doubling his allotted amount, which meant he'd been consuming almost as much as he should, and he seemed to be doing fine. For my part, I could afford to cut back. I could stick to my originally allotted amount for meals, save the extra we'd packed for Dash, as well as all of the snacks.

I looked at our remaining stores, but still the math didn't come out. No matter how much I cut down my portions, there was no way we'd make it three days. Just no way. We'd essentially be hiking the last day without food.

"Okay," I said. "We have an issue. I'm going to have to go pretty lean."

"Okay," he said. "I can stop eating so much, too."

I felt a ridiculous welling of affection for him at that moment. He didn't freak out, and he was game to do what needed to be done.

"Nope," I said. "You eat what you need."

His brow furrowed and he shook his head. "How is that fair?"

"Aside from the fact that this is my mistake?" I said, smiling. "You're nothing but muscle and bone already. I've got stores." I patted my belly. "And also 'cause I'm the dad."

"But—"

"No buts. You eat what you need. I'll be okay."

"No way."

"Seriously, Dash. That's what fat is for. It's for times like this. I'm carrying extra fuel." I patted my less-than-washboard stomach. "You're not. If you don't eat, you'll bonk. I won't."

"I'll what?"

"It's a marathoner's term. It happened to me once. In training, I ran a full marathon-length run two weeks out. I was super fit at the time, so I was feeling invincible. I took off that morning with only a handful of Shot Blocks."

"What's a Shot Block?"

"Giant gummy bears, essentially. Long story short, I ate about two hundred calories and I burned over two thousand. At about the eighteen-mile marker, my energy cratered. I could barely lift my legs. I only made it another five miles before I had to shuffle the last three miles home."

"Yikes. Did you call Mom to get you?"

"Too embarrassed."

That brought a smile to his lips. "I bet."

"And that's not going to happen to you," I said.

He looked a little rebellious, but he didn't argue. I realized I was going to have to watch him to make sure he ate enough.

I felt like an idiot for not thinking this through ahead of time, and I swore I wasn't going to make that mistake again once we got back to civilization. I'd just have to tough it out on that last day, that's all. I'd gone on fasts before. The body is a pretty amazing thing, and if it was only for one day, I'd be okay. It wouldn't be pleasant, but it'd be doable.

I packed up the rest of the food, stuffed it in the bear bag along with our toothbrushes and toothpaste.

"Did you get all the snacks and snack wrappers out of your pack?" I asked. His pack's belt had two little pouches on it where he liked to keep in-hike snacks, and he was less than diligent about emptying those pouches. This wouldn't have been a huge problem if he hadn't also taken to putting his pack inside the tent to use as a pillow.

The last thing we wanted was to have tasty-smelling food or wrappers inside the tent if a bear wandered by.

"Yep. Checked 'em," he said.

I rolled down the top of the bear bag, pushed out the air, rolled it up tighter, then clicked the clasp.

Our bear bag was a river rafting dry bag, what my research on the internet had said was most commonly used to keep food out of reach from bears when hiking in the woods. The notion is to put all your food—plus anything that might give off a food-like scent—into a bag, go far away from your tent or anyone else's, and hoist the bag high up enough that a bear can't get it. Common wisdom says ten feet up and six feet out on a limb.

After loading the bag, the next step is to find a good tree—one at least two hundred feet away from any tents—to hang the bag. Now you've got your tree selected, you've got your bag ready, so...how does one get a forty-pound bear bag ten feet up in the air and six feet out on a limb? Well, it's like an elementary school science project with rocks and string.

One of the things on Megan's sister's magic list was parachute cord. I had never heard of parachute cord. I had certainly never considered taking it on a camping trip.

But if you ever have to hang a bear bag, get parachute cord. It's lightweight and strong. The line I used was about the same thickness as standard twine, but it hefted that forty-pound bag like an inch-thick rope. It never broke, not even after five weeks of being thrown over limbs and yanked across rough bark.

But perhaps the most amazing part about parachute cord—and probably the reason it is chosen by backpackers over any other cord—is that it's magically slick. It doesn't get caught on all the tiny dead branches sticking out from a tree trunk like a porcupine's quills, or on the ragged grooves between plates of bark.

So I went to hang the bear bag. I found a nice big branch over ten feet up. I found a chunk of granite big enough to carry the line up and over the limb, small enough that I could lob it that far. I created a horizontal and vertical loop around the rock with the parachute cord and cinched it tight.

Next was the tricky part. In the midst of sleep deprivation, tender feet, the descending cold, and the dream of getting into my sleeping bag, I had to lob the rock just so. If I missed the first time, starting over again had a whole new set of problems I now knew from experience. Yank the stone back too hard and the rock would jump over another branch and get stuck. Or the knot could come loose in the fall and I'd have to spend time retying the damned rock. Or, the fear of every bear-bag-hanging enthusiast, the line could get stuck up there. Really stuck.

This was why parachute cord was a godsend. It was miraculously designed to slither through all but the most tangled situations.

I cocked my arm back and…I lobbed the line correctly on the first try.

Booya! That was a first for me, and a nice little victory for the day. On the previous nights, between hunting for the perfect branch and making the throw correctly, hanging the bear bag had sometimes taken me up to thirty minutes.

I attached the bag to the line, hauled it up and tied it off. With the bear bag safe and secure, I hobbled back to the tent.

In the light of the setting sun, I found Dash talking to a pair of hikers. They were both young—probably in their late twenties—and Dash was holding a handful of big colorful packets.

"Dad," Dash said. "This is Steven and Kelly."

"Hi." I greeted them warmly. "Nice to meet you."

"They gave us food!" Dash said, holding up the packets, which were three pre-made dehydrated meals: a scrambled egg breakfast hash, a Pad Thai noodle dinner, and an Italian linguine dinner.

I suddenly wondered what Dash had said to them. He shouldn't go begging food from other campers. "Dash, you didn't—"

"No! I didn't say a thing. I swear. They just came over."

"We packed too much food," Steven said. "We're off the trail at the end of the segment tomorrow, and we've got way too much. Can't use it after, so I came over to see if you wanted it."

"You're kidding," I said.

"Why, you low on food?" Kelly asked.

"As a matter of fact, we are. We just did the math and it was going to be a lean last few days before Breckenridge."

"Perfect." Steven beamed. "I'm glad I came over."

I laughed and hooked a thumb at Dash. "Not as glad as this guy, I can tell you." Dash was still grinning at the food in his hands. "You saved us from some hunger pangs."

It was freaky in the best sort of way. Kinda makes one believe that the Universe was looking out for us.

Before the sun fell, the campsite filled up with a dozen other hikers. Obviously this was a planned stopping point for quite a few people. It was strange. When we were hiking the trail, I'd rarely seen another hiker. But a great campsite like this collected hikers like a bend in a river collects driftwood, and that night it became apparent for the first time that there were lots of people hiking the CT.

That night I slept worse than the previous two. There were plenty of tents nearby, and Dash wasn't the only one who snored. Geez...

I tossed and turned, listened to my audio book. I dozed, only to be awoken time and again. Finally, at about five in the morning, I gave up.

I rolled out of the tent to a stunning moon hanging low over the dark mountains. It was so bright it seemed like some alternate kind of daylight, like I was on an alien planet. The glow lit the meadow, brushing the tall grass with pale light, and the river below was a sparkling silver ribbon.

"Man..." I murmured to myself. Again, I took pictures, and they did absolutely no justice to the moment. But the glorious scene took my mind off my fatigue and the pain in my feet. I felt lucky to be able to witness it.

After attempting to rouse Dash a dozen times—this would become a theme—we broke camp and began hiking. Dash began working out our new eating schedule. He'd taken to the calorie problem with zest, and he took charge of food rationing. He figured how much each of us could eat in a day until we reached Breckenridge, which was still three days away. The three meals Steven and Kelly had given us would help, but hadn't fixed the problem. We wouldn't starve completely on the last day, but we'd still be running at a significant calorie deficit. It made me proud to see him take charge like that, thinking about these things on his own, being proactive and working on the solution.

For my part, I had a new problem. I'd taken a portable charger for my phone that I'd been using to recharge it, but I'd used up all its juice already. All I had left was a seventy-five percent charge on my phone itself. That wasn't going to be enough to reach Breckenridge. It'd barely be enough to last until sunset tomorrow, even if I turned it off altogether. Cold nights in the mountains can dull a battery pretty quickly. I was still contemplating what to do about that.

Our goal for the day was thirteen miles, but after just two of those, my feet were hurting badly. I couldn't walk a step without shooting pain. All told, we had come just over fifty miles so far. If my feet didn't start to get better, there was simply no way I could hike another four hundred.

"Dash," I said at noon as we ate our allotted Clif Bar and tuna packet. "I have to make you aware of something."

He glanced over at me.

"My feet are pretty bad. I just… I don't know if I can keep doing this."

"Your blisters?"

"I'm just saying I'm in a bit of pain here, and it's not getting better. I was hoping my feet would toughen up, but they're getting worse."

"What does that mean?" he asked. I watched the realization dawn in his eyes. He glanced at my feet.

"I'm just… I don't know if I can hike the entire trail if my feet don't get better. I don't think I'll physically be able to do it."

"But Dad…no," he said. "Now that I'm out here, I want to finish. This is amazing."

I'd jumped into The Colorado Trail with fervor, but as had been my way in my youth, I had meant to test it out, see how it went, and take things one step at a time. I mean, I'd meant to finish it if we could, but I'd had doubts we'd make it that far.

Except I'd assumed it'd be Dash who'd want to quit, not me.

In fact, I'd been so certain he would hit a wall of disinterest that I'd exacted a promise from him before we started the trail. I'd told him we had to hike at least the first two weeks, that we absolutely couldn't quit until we'd crossed that threshold. I'd figured once we passed that mark, he'd have the best chance to get accustomed to the trail enough to want to finish.

We'd shook on it.

Now, looking into his earnest face, my commitment galvanized. I didn't need to hike the entire CT for myself, but I realized I would rather die than be the one to let Dash down. I wasn't going to quit because of mere discomfort. My feet would literally have to stop working before I'd throw in the towel.

My perspective shifted. Rather than thinking "how can I make this pain stop?" I wondered how far I could push myself before I simply couldn't walk anymore.

"You got it, buddy," I said. "We'll keep going. I swear I won't give up. If I can physically keep going, I will." The suddenness and ferocity of my resolve surprised even me.

He nodded, but there was also a bit of worry on his face. I think he realized for the first time how much pain I was in.

After that perspective shift, I discovered a whole new gear. Yes, my feet hurt. Yes, every step was painful, but the pain became a sliding scale. I told myself that this was simply the way it was now. This was the new normal. I had painful feet, and that was that.

I plodded toward the horizon one wince at a time.

10

THE GREAT FARTING

THAT NIGHT WE DRY CAMPED, which is camping without a nearby water source. The first thing I did after dropping my pack was to pull my feet out of the Cruel Shoes and slip them into my blessed Crocs. It felt like a massage for my feet.

I shuffled around, setting up the tent and getting the food out as quickly as I could. The sun had started to set, and the temperature was dropping. We were racing against time. Within moments, I had put on every layer I owned to trap my warmth.

Ever since we'd talked about the state of my feet, Dash had kept an eye on me. He also leapt to do everything he could. He helped me set up the tent. He got the stove going and set up dinner. We wolfed it down, then he helped me wash the dishes and stow everything. I hung the bear bag, then we jumped into the tent and snuggled into our sleeping bags.

I, for one, was really looking forward to sleeping. After three nights of almost zero sleep, I had reached a fatigue threshold that promised to knock me unconscious no matter how loud the snoring.

As the tent warmed up and the chill seeped out of my bones, Dash and I lay there talking, reviewing the wonders we'd already seen. Our Kelty tent had actually turned out to be amazing at trapping body heat, and as it warmed up, I felt a pleasant lassitude. My body sank into my sleeping pad...

And the tent suddenly filled with noxious gas.

Now, maybe it was having eaten Clif Bars, almonds, and tuna for four days straight, or maybe it was the vegetarian dehydrated bean and jalapeño mix we'd just scarfed down, but...

Oh. My. God.

I ignored it. I mean, the tent was so small that Dash and I were nearly touching. It seemed bad form to comment on our collective silent-but-deadlies.

Dash stayed fixated on his phone, which still had some battery, and seemed not to notice. Or maybe he was just playing the same courtesy game that I was.

I put in my Airpods and tried to focus on the audio book *Hyperion* by Dan Simmons.

The noxious cloud worsened, which I actually hadn't thought possible. I concentrated on ignoring it. Dash didn't say a thing.

I shifted, trying to find a way to get comfortable. We didn't carry pillows with us, so my pillow was my spongy blue fleece, wadded up and stuck underneath my neck.

As I'd mentioned before, Dash had taken to bringing his backpack into the tent as a pillow after the second night proved his rainfly to be less than effective at keeping his stuff dry. It was far too tall a pillow for me, but Dash liked it.

The fart smell worsened. It was like someone had tossed a military-grade stink bomb into our tent. I thought my eyes would start watering. Good God! I was going to have to throw open the tent flap. Can a person asphyxiate from human methane?

I turned away from Dash with a grunt. I was sure he had generated the bulk of the cloud. In retrospect, I imagine he was sure *I* had.

"I've come up with our trail name," Dash said into the tense quiet.

"*Our* trail name?" I responded quickly. I didn't want my mouth open too long in that unbreathable air.

"The Shhhhtinky Onion Man!" he exclaimed.

We were both silent for half a second, then we burst into laughter. We laughed so hard, tears rolled down our faces. We laughed so hard and for so long, I pulled out my camera and took selfies while we were still giggling.

There is one picture—which I would later post on Facebook—that is my favorite of all time. There isn't a better bonding picture of me and my son anywhere. Perhaps there isn't a better bonding picture of any dad and son.

Because of farts. Good lord...

After our grand laughing, we aired out the tent and tried to simmer down, though the giggles kept catching us at random moments. I checked my phone and, by some miracle, our campsite had cell service. We celebrated by calling Lara and delivering a chaotic rush of everything we'd done. Including the Great Farting.

It was wonderful to talk to her and just hear her voice and the noises of home in the background. Galahad's bark. Elo's voice asking who was on the phone. Food cooking and the faucet running.

And toward the end of the call, we begged for food.

The Data Book—which by now we had both learned to read—told us we were coming up on Kenosha Pass tomorrow, where the CT intersected Highway 285. There aren't too many places the CT intersects such an easy access point, and it was the perfect spot to maybe get some extra supplies two days before our scheduled resupply in Breckenridge. We asked Lara if she might consider spending an afternoon to come meet us at the Kenosha Pass campgrounds and bring us emergency food. I also asked her to bring emergency moleskin for me.

That angel from on high said she would.

That night, Dash slept well as usual. Unfortunately for me, I didn't get the rest I'd hoped for. I tossed and turned, trying to find some rhythm within the snoring and turn it into white noise, but there was simply no way. I finally put my Airpods back in, turned the volume up and tried to let the story be my white noise.

It sort of worked. I slept at times, but if Dash's snoring shifted gears too abruptly, or if the audio book suddenly had a suspenseful part that got noisy, I popped to the surface of consciousness. The result was that I seemed to have a lot of half-waking dreams, and most of them were bizarre, related to the worlds of Simmons' *Hyperion*. Mucking through the mud pits of Mars. Fleeing from the Shrike.

We got up the next morning and headed out, but I was dragging. I fell into the rhythm of painful walking. I had a closer end point now, and it gave me hope. In one day, I might find some bit of relief. Certainly we would fix the food problem, but maybe I'd also be able to fix my feet with something Lara would bring—moleskin, corn pads or whatever.

We hiked all day in the heat, and we reached the end of Segment 5 ready to drink our fill. According to the Data Book, there was a prime water source at the end of the segment, otherwise known as a "Full Cup." In the book, three icons represented forthcoming water sources:
- A Full Cup—plenty of water, either a strong-flowing stream, a full fledged river, or a spigot like at the fire house
- A Half Cup—a little creek or a spring that was probably running
- An Empty Cup with an exclamation point—which meant "Rely on it if you like, dude. It flows in the spring, but the sucker's probably dry now."

When we hiked into the dusty, packed-dirt parking lot, about a tenth of a mile east of Highway 285, which I could see in the distance, we found a restroom, a lot full of RVs...

...but no obvious water source. My old city fears rushed back, that the Data Book had let us down. But that couldn't be right. It just couldn't. The Data Book had been spot-on every other time. It was just a matter of understanding what was on the page.

Dash spotted Steven—one of the hikers who had given us food last night—sitting by a sign at the edge of the parking lot, so he went over to say hello. I turned around in that dusty parking lot like some character in a survival movie, casting about for the promised water.

Dash came back quickly. Apparently Steven hadn't been in much of a talking mood, so Dash had thanked him for the food again and left.

That's when it clicked in my brain.

"We're on the wrong side of the highway," I said. I looked down the long dirt road, at the end of which I could barely see the highway. It hadn't occurred to me that there would be two campgrounds in this spot, one for RVs and one for car camping. I peered into the distance. On the far side of the highway was another parking lot, and trees beyond. There could very well be a campground on the other side.

"This isn't the right place?" Dash asked.

"Can't be," I said.

"Why?"

"Because the Data Book says there's a water source, and there's no water." Rather than doubting the book, I doubted that I'd read it correctly, just like at the volunteer fire station. We just hadn't walked far enough. "I'm betting we have to cross the highway," I said.

"Cool," Dash said. Camel that he was, he wasn't suffering much from the lack of water.

"Well," I said. "We're not going to find water hanging around here." I started up the dirt road in the bright sun.

It was a relatively short hike down the dirt road, but it was hot and dusty. After hiking through the glorious deep woods and over beautiful ridges with vistas that stole my breath, hiking up an old dirt road just sucked.

But we made it to the highway, played real-life Frogger with the traffic—it's amazing how little time we had to scurry across the road when cars were whistling along at seventy miles per hour—and made it to the other side.

I was right. The sign read:

KENOSHA PARK CAMPGROUND

It was a pay campsite, and it cost twenty-two dollars. After having plopped down our tent wherever we liked for free for the past five nights, that suddenly seemed outrageously expensive. I hadn't planned to pay for camping at all during this trip. Originally—before we ran out of food—the plan was to get water at this site and hike another three miles to our final destination for the night. But now that sounded ludicrous. We'd have to hike to the campsite, drop our tent, hike back, meet with Lara, then hike back to the campsite. It would add another nine miles to the day.

That was not happening.

I paid the twenty-two dollars, found the water, set up camp, and lounged about, waiting. The amazing campsite hosts even let me plug into their RV outlet and charge up my dead phone.

When Lara arrived at five o'clock, I had my feet up on the picnic table. The skies had clouded and a light drizzle had begun, but Dash and I just flipped up our rain jackets and didn't worry about it. We'd gotten used to the fickle weather of the trail.

Lara had brought our sixteen-year-old daughter Elowyn and our brand-new, not-even-a-year-old Weimaraner, Galahad.

He burst out of the van with overwhelming exuberance, leaping on me, then sniffing everything he could sniff, then running back to leap on me all over again. It buoyed my spirits just to see him. Dogs are amazing that way. No matter what you're going through, they always find a way to make you feel better.

Once the dog had dominated my attention for that frantic moment, I turned and hugged Elo and Lara. I had never been so happy to see two people. After hugs, Dash pulled Elo toward our tent, telling her stories from the trail.

Lara had noticed my limp, and her face filled with concern. "Honey, are you okay?" She followed me as I hobbled away to hang the bear bag. It took us a distance from the kids and the dog.

I've heard that dogs will often be stoic in front of their pack mates. Weakness could translate to getting left behind or, in some cases, being outright attacked. So injured dogs will often pretend nothing's wrong. For those dog owners out there, you may have experienced this. My previous Weimaraner, Lancelot, once nearly de-gloved his front paw—yes, it's exactly as gross as you're imagining—but he acted like he didn't even notice. When we took him to the vet and they put him alone in the room with only a camera to monitor him, he began whining and whimpering the moment they closed the door.

I felt a bit like that now. I'd put on a game face for Dash, but with Lara, I let my guard down. As soon as we were out of earshot, I leaned on her and said, "God, it hurts so bad."

"Honey, maybe you should stop. I talked to Dr. Hones and he said you need to be really careful those blisters don't get infected. If they do, you're done. There won't be any more hiking this year. Maybe you should take a break now, instead of where you'd planned."

"No." I shook my head. "We've got one more segment to Breckenridge. Then I can give my feet a rest."

"Honey, that segment is thirty-three miles long."

"I'm going to finish out the week."

"Honey—"

"I promised Dash. I can make it."

She looked dubious.

"It's actually not so bad once I get moving," I said. "It's when I stop that it gets a little overwhelming. I just needed to whine about it for a second. I'm good."

She shook her head and frowned.

"I am," I promised. "I'm okay."

"Let's get out of this rain and eat," she said.

"You're going to eat with us?" I asked.

"Come on."

We all gathered into the van, and it had the juicy, succulent, sizzling aroma of a restaurant.

"Oh, what did you do?" I asked.

She smiled at me.

"Thought you might like this," Elo said, holding up two giant bags.

They had brought a feast of fresh Mexican food.

"Oh, I love you guys so much!" Dash exclaimed.

We leapt on those chimichangas like lions on an antelope. It was dead silent in that van for a good two minutes as Dash and I stuffed our faces. In addition to all the other supplies we'd requested—extra food, a roll of moleskin, corn pads, and Neosporin—they'd brought a deep fried dinner, something impossible to get on the trail. It was heaven. I couldn't remember the last time I'd been so satisfied by a meal. We ate and ate and ate until we simply couldn't eat anymore, and still there was food left.

Afterward, we said our goodbyes, and Lara, Elo, and Galahad got back into the car to return to the luxury of city life—sleep that lasted the whole night, bellies full of whatever food you wanted. I had mixed feelings as they drove away. I had abandoned my chance to skip the upcoming thirty-three-mile, foot-stabbing ordeal. On the other hand, I now felt a strange sense of pride. I was going to stick it out, and while my head counseled caution, my heart was all in.

Now I'll let you in on a little secret and a big secret.

The little secret is really no secret at all to those who know me: I have a commitment phobia. With friends, with businesses, with strangers, I am reluctant to commit unless I absolutely have to. Even with social engagements, I equivocate and avoid making solid plans until the last minute.

So yeah. I don't fill up my calendar on a whim. It's not something I even do consciously, just a knee-jerk aversion. You have to pin me down, squirming, to get a promise out of me.

But if I actually *do* give you a commitment, I'm all in. I'll take it to the end of the line. Sometimes obsessively so.

That's the little secret. Here's the big one: There's a reason for my commitment phobia and its rare, obsessive flipside: a deep scar from my childhood that shaped my personality.

It has to do with the two rabbits I killed when I was ten years old.

11
TWO DEAD RABBITS

When I was ten years old, back at the beginning of the flamboyant 1980s, I lived in a house on a mesa. Florida Mesa is about eleven miles outside of Durango, and our two-story house sat on three acres of land. It's the only place, before my current house in Englewood, that I've ever really called home.

When I think of my childhood, I think of those open fields and their barbed wire fences, posts gray and weathered by time. I remember the friendly old horses in the field across the road where the girl next door, who *everybody* had a crush on, lived.

And at the end of the road of our subdivision lived a boy named Danny. He was a year younger than me, which seemed like a lot at the time, but we had mutual interests: Dungeons and Dragons, comic books, riding our dirt bikes all over the place, playing the latest at-home video games like *Pitfall* and Atari's *Raiders of the Lost Ark*, and sitting in rapt attention around the circular game board of the supremely cool, partially electronic Dark Tower (God that thing was awesome!).

Anyway, one day during the summer of 1980, Danny and I

were kicking around in a pile of boards and pipes in his back yard by the pond. Just beyond that small industrial bone yard was a giant willow tree that was great for climbing. And that's where we were headed, to spend time in its cool branches and talk about those super important things that ten-year-olds talk about.

Of course, we both had sticks. Summer wasn't summer without a stick in my hand. And I, of course, pretended that stick was a sword. I always did. Everything in my life was about fantasy. Or if it wasn't about fantasy, I tried to *make* it about fantasy. I viewed life through this imaginative lens: I wasn't actually walking in Danny's back yard with a stick. I was a knight errant, exploring the countryside, seeking a quest.

That's just the way I looked at the world back then.

Hell, I guess I still do.

Anyway, as we were clambering over the debris on the way to the willow, a rabbit popped up from between two pipes and sprinted away from us.

I can't describe the sudden, light-headed feel of the chase. I never consciously chose to chase that rabbit. It just happened. A relatively dull moment became bright with purpose. I honestly don't know who leapt after the rabbit first, me or Danny, but suddenly we were on the hunt.

Danny actually *was* a hunter. He owned a rifle, and he and his father had gone to hunt deer before. Me? I'd never hunted anything in my short life, though I did understand what guns were. My dad had three of them, high up in the closet. One .22 caliber rifle and two handguns: a 9mm semiautomatic and .22 caliber revolver. I remember the revolver was zipped into a green velvet sleeve the color of felt on a pool table. I'd even seen my dad shoot the guns, though never at anything but cans.

Looking back, I didn't think about whether I was an experienced hunter or not. I didn't think about anything. I only remember my instinct to reach the rabbit.

Danny and I were pretty well matched physically, but this time I was faster. I stayed right behind the rabbit as it darted into a pipe. I raced above it, tiptoes striking the top of the curved pipe as deftly as a circus performer on a tight wire. I was sure the rabbit was going to come out the far side.

And I was right. I reached the end just as the rabbit shot out of the pipe, trying to make for the wide-open field.

But I was close enough now. I had that rabbit.

And I had a stick.

I brought it down on the rabbit's back with all my might, and I heard the snap…

And that's when the whole world changed.

That bright purpose, that hot rush, suddenly vanished. One moment, I was at the forefront of a divine race, wings on my feet, wielding my mighty stick-sword…

The next moment I was watching this graceful, scared creature twitching, trying to run without the ability to do so. I froze in place and dropped my stick. The world had turned ugly and horribly real. I'd hurt the rabbit. I'd hurt it really bad.

I wanted to vomit. I wanted to cry. I wanted to scream, "No!" and undo it. But I just stood there, gaping.

"What are you doing?" Danny demanded.

"I didn't want… I didn't want to do that…" I stuttered, unable to take my eyes off the poor rabbit, still struggling to get to its feet with a broken back.

"You can't just let it suffer like that," Danny said. I turned my glazed expression on him, and I was stunned to realize he wasn't horrified by what I'd done. It was like there were rules about this sort of thing, that killing the creature wasn't wrong. But letting it suffer was.

He moved past me, and I turned away as he finished the job.

I'd been exultant right up to the moment of the strike. I'd wanted…something I couldn't define. I'd wanted it so badly it had taken me past my ability to understand what I was doing. It had taken me past my humanity. That was my first experience with bloodlust.

It sickened me to know I had that ability to destroy, so close to the surface. And I was not only capable of destroying, but I was good at it. I'd moved faster than Danny. I'd anticipated better. I'd struck with force, accuracy, and zero hesitation.

For the first time, I was scared of myself. I was afraid of what I might do if I didn't control my own actions. That rushing heat had been a kind of euphoria, and I'd liked it. It had seemed natural.

I decided right then that I never wanted to be a hunter, that I could never, ever let that violence out again. Not like that. Unsupervised. Uncontrolled. Free to strike and kill.

I didn't see Danny take that rabbit inside. Didn't even see him pick it up. I couldn't look at him, couldn't stand the thought that he would see my shame. I ran home. I couldn't get away from that place fast enough, and though I'd return to Danny's house many times in later months and years, I would never return to the bone yard or to the willow tree.

Danny's family actually skinned and ate the rabbit that night. They had it for dinner because they didn't believe in wasting food. I tried to tell myself that made it better. It should have made it better. It didn't.

That event forced a decision in my mind, a fork in the path of my development. It wasn't a conscious one, but it was a concrete one: I wasn't going to be a violent man.

Maybe there was no way to stop that heated desire to chase, to use my body for violence, but I could at least control it. I could bleed that desire out in other ways, like chopping wood for my dad, or in the physical rigors of dance in college, or under the discipline of martial arts in my forties. But not on animals. Not on people. Not ever again.

I'd seen the monster inside, and no one else was ever going to see it. No one I loved would ever have cause to fear me.

I wish I could say that was the only rabbit I ever killed. It's not. There were two.

The second rabbit didn't die through violence, but it changed my life more profoundly than the first, I think.

The second rabbit showed me something about myself

that scared me in a different way, in an insidious way that made me wonder if I could ever really trust myself at all. I mean, it's far easier to notice when you're raising a stick over your head than to realize you're neglecting a responsibility.

But the consequences of neglect can be just as final.

It was a hard, personal lesson, though not so dramatic. There wasn't a wild chase, a rabbit running for his life. This rabbit had been my pet.

In fifth grade, we had a class rabbit. When summer came around, the rabbit needed a new home, and the teacher chose me. I was exultant. I loved animals, dogs and cats, all kinds of animals. I was a pretty sensitive kid, and I had a knack for getting animals to trust me. Getting to have my very own pet was like a dream come true.

My mother told me I'd be responsible for caring for it. For feeding it and watering it, for playing with it and cleaning its cage, and I accepted that responsibility without thinking—without knowing—what it really meant. I just wanted the rabbit.

Dad built a little hutch in the barn with chicken wire for walls and a plexiglass floor and top. The top had a handle I could easily open, so I could take the bunny out to play or give it food and water. For two weeks, all I did was play with that bunny. I religiously cleaned the cage and checked its food and water twice a day. My brother and sister were jealous that I had my own pet, but I let them play with it as much as they wanted, so the jealousy didn't last.

After the first month, the excitement faded, and I fell into the routine, but with less enthusiasm. I didn't take the bunny out to play as much, but I still cleaned out the cage and brought it food and water. The summer wore on, and I visited less and less. I remember my mother reminding me regularly to make sure I took care of my bunny responsibilities. Every time she did, I did as asked.

One morning, I woke up in a panic.

It was late November and winter had left a dusting of snow on the mesa. My heart pounded like I'd had a nightmare, but I couldn't remember what it was. My brother slept silently across from me in the room we shared. I got up, shivered, and went to the window. The sun peeked over the eastern horizon, lighting the high, cold clouds with lemon yellow. The driveway below and the fields beyond were dark.

Why was I scared? Why was I...?

My rabbit.

My nameless terror coalesced into certainty. I knew what had awoken me. I couldn't remember the last time my mother had reminded me to take care of my rabbit. I couldn't remember. That meant it had been days. And it had been even longer since I'd visited the rabbit, since I'd gone out to the barn.

"No no no..." I murmured. I pushed my feet into my slippers, ran up the hall, unlocked the front door and burst onto the porch. I barely kept my feet as I skidded down the snow-covered stairs and bolted for the barn.

I remember the darkness of the barn, the smell of dust and cold, and the little bunny's corpse on the plexiglass floor of the hutch. In that first split-second, I told myself the bunny had frozen, that he hadn't been warm enough. That it wasn't my fault he was dead. But I knew that was a lie. He'd died because I forgot about him, because I was a horrible caretaker. He'd died of thirst, starved to death because no one came to help him.

Later—I don't know how much later—my mom found me on my knees in the barn in my pajamas in the freezing cold, crying. She tried to pull me away, and I yelled that I'd killed my bunny, I'd killed my bunny.

I never got over that. I hadn't taken a stick to that rabbit, but I'd killed it just as surely. I'd taken charge of the well-being of another living creature, and I'd failed.

As I became a young man, graduating from high school and adventuring out into the world, I avoided responsibility like the plague. I kept no pets. Not ever. And I did my best to minimize situations where people had to rely on me. I was intense and breezy with friends by turn. I loved deep, late-night conversations, but I avoided committing to anything. I became the Teflon man.

I was terrified of letting anybody down because I was a horrible caretaker. Oh, I was a fun guy. I could light up a room with enthusiasm. But through deeds and words, I kept my non-stick surface, giving an unspoken warning that I shouldn't be counted upon.

Want to catch a movie with me? Better ask me last minute. If you put out a call a week in advance, I'll joke around with you, leave you with a smile, but I won't give you a commitment.

I did a lot of traveling in my twenties. I hitchhiked across the U.S., road tripped everywhere there was a road, and I never stayed in one place for more than a year. When it came to girls, I had perfected my Teflon speech, and I always delivered it before I progressed to anything physical. It went something like this, "Hey, I'm here. You're here. If you want to have fun, I'm all for it. But I could be gone tomorrow. If you've got an agenda, you're going to be disappointed. At a certain point, I *will* leave. If that doesn't work for you, let's just shake hands and be friends."

I was protecting them. I felt like I was giving them a head-start to get away from me if a simple, no-strings roll-in-the-hay wasn't enough. I mean, it wasn't easy for me to put the brakes on in those situations. I really wanted to jump in bed, but I'd stop. Rather than letting the heat of the moment sweep me away, *then* explaining my lifestyle after I'd gotten what I wanted, I put my cards on the table up front.

With jobs, it was painful to pin my squirming soul down and commit to deadlines. It's still painful. Even today, I waffle and struggle every time I choose a deadline for one of my novels. And I far prefer to have a novel absolutely, completely finished before I pick a publication date, just so I don't promise something I'm not positive I can deliver.

When I do finally commit to something, though, I commit all the way. It's like all those years of breezy non-commitment were creating reserves that I could pour into the one or two things that really mattered to me.

In 2003, when I decided to leave my gypsy life behind, I planted both feet and I didn't move. All that worry about hurting those I loved, about neglecting them, about letting them down, all came pouring out of me like wet concrete into the mold of the foundation that would stand for the rest of my life.

That year, I proposed to Lara, we got two dogs, we bought a house, we got married, and we had a baby.

I've never looked back. In fact, I'd bet those who have met me in the past ten years probably have a hard time imagining me as anything other than a family man.

So, when I made my commitment to Dash about The Colorado Trail, it was that kind of commitment. I was in it now, body and soul. My feet would actually have to fall off for me to quit. They'd have to put me in the hospital.

And my feet hadn't failed yet. Until then, I was doing this trail, and that was the end of that.

So while one might assume I felt a sense of dread as Lara drove away, I didn't. I actually felt relaxed. The temptation was gone, and it lightened my mind. It made things simple.

"You okay, Dad?" Dash asked as he came up next to me.

I smiled. "I'm good, buddy. Let's get some sleep. Big day tomorrow."

12

GEORGIA PASS

THE NEXT SEGMENT was thirty-two-point-seven miles long. That's a goodly distance on healthy feet, and it's even longer when trying to levitate on the lip-biting pain flowers my feet had become. After all, while my commitment was as firm as polished stone, the difficulty of my situation was still red and raw.

I hadn't been lying to Lara when I'd told her the pain became tolerable once I got moving. Maybe it was because of increased blood flow, or maybe once my body realized I wasn't going to listen to the pain signals, it sent out a numbing agent to help me soldier on. Or maybe it was just the distraction of the breathtaking beauty over every rise. I don't know. Whatever the case, the pain was manageable.

As we hiked, Dash now took the lead more often than not, and at about four miles down the trail, as I had sunk into a churning rhythm, he had ranged about twenty feet ahead of me.

I was lost in my own little world, dreaming of tonight's campsite and my blessed Crocs, which dangled and swung from the back of my pack.

At this point, it's important to note that The Colorado Trail isn't just for hikers. There are a lot of mountain bikers, too. We'd quickly learned the social protocol: if you see a cyclist coming, step off to the side and let them zip by.

The official trail rules—and multiple posted signs—state that cyclists must give way to hikers, but that makes little sense when it's far easier for a hiker to take one step to the side than it is for a biker to break off the trail, churn up a slope then down it, and hop back on the trail. Stepping off only takes a second, and the cyclists will usually smile and throw a quick thank you as they zoom past.

At any rate, I heard a cyclist coming behind me. I brought myself out of my zone and stepped to the side. But instead of whooshing past me, he braked. The guy was handsome and robust with a mane of wavy black hair.

I blinked, drawing myself out of my internal dreamland. "Everything okay?" I asked.

"Yeah. I think I have something for you," he said. A single silver Croc hung from his handlebar. "I saw it on the trail, figured someone might be missing it."

My heart lurched and I grappled frantically behind me to touch my Crocs. Sure enough, one was missing, and it was sitting right there on this guy's handlebars.

"Oh my God!" I said. "Thank you." Not having my Crocs when we reached camp was a barely conceivable notion. What would I have done? The only thing that kept me plodding forward, one painful foot at a time, was the idea that I could take off the Cruel Shoes when I got to camp and put on my cushy Crocs.

"You're a life saver," I continued to gush. "Thank you. Thank you so much."

He handed the Croc over, grinning. By then, I had taken off my pack. I'd thought my Crocs had been secure, but I must not have put the heel straps all the way into the carabiner. It hadn't clicked shut.

The cyclist's name was Genaro, and we chatted for

another minute as I profusely thanked him over and over, then he smiled and waved and headed off on his journey.

With effusive gratitude to the gods of trail angels, I kissed my fingers and turned them to the sky. That was a disaster narrowly avoided through the kindness of a stranger.

Dash and I continued on, hiking our first big peak of the journey, but I nervously kept reaching back to touch my Crocs. In fact, I would go on to make periodic checks like that for the rest of the entire journey.

We'd started at six thousand feet at the beginning of Segment 2, and we'd gained thousands of feet of elevation since then. But on our sixth day, we took our first trip above tree line—the point at which it's too high for trees to grow— over Georgia Pass. The peak tops out at eleven thousand eight hundred and seventy-four feet.

The view? Wow. What can I say? We could see forever. Layers upon layers of mountains stacked up in the distance, just like that first night standing next to Gretchen, except now the mountains were all half-bathed in sunlight and half in shadow. It was hard to encompass just how much land we could see all at once from the height of nearly twelve thousand feet. We were so high up, I could see different weather systems. Bright sunshine over that cluster of peaks. Dark storm clouds over that one. I could even see sheets of rain coming down far to the southwest, including little flickers of lightning.

As I stood there catching my breath, consumed by the beauty of it all, a different realization struck me. That storm was far away. But how long would it take to get here? Certainly storms could move faster than people. How far were we from the safety of the tree line on the other side of this peak?

Between all the other things that had occupied my time on the trail—lending inspiration to my son to get up steep inclines, learning to read the Data Book, sorting out our food problem, staying dry, and babying my feet—I hadn't given much thought to the hazards of going above tree line.

I thought about it now, and figured we should keep moving. We came down off the peak pretty quickly and into the relative safety of the trees on the far side. About that time, it began to drizzle.

We donned our rain gear and I didn't think another thing about lightning.

Dash hiked down the trail with gusto—he loved declines—and I limped after. That afternoon, we made it to a wooded campground near North Fork Swan River. Lots of flat spaces, a tasty water source, protective pines, and enough time for us to set up and watch the sun set.

It was in this campground that we met Brian, the first hiker upon whom we would bestow a trail name: Smiley.

Dash and I had gotten into the trail name game after we'd miraculously met Gretchen a second time late during Segment 3. She'd paused to appreciate a spot she'd particularly liked, unwittingly giving us time to catch up to her, and we had hobnobbed for a while at the intersection of the trail and an old Jeep road. During this conversation, she'd said she had come up with a trail name for me.

"Since you're an epic fantasy writer," she had said, "I thought of Epic for your trail name."

I, of course, loved it. What's not to love?

"I didn't come up with one for you," she had said to Dash. "Because, let's face it, 'Dash' is a pretty awesome trail name already."

Since that moment, Dash and I thought hard about what trail name to give Gretchen the next time we saw her. We finally decided her trail name should be "Fleet" because of how fleet-footed she was. We were truly excited to bestow this upon her the next time we met. Unfortunately, we never saw Gretchen again.

So, Gretchen, if you're reading this and you haven't gotten your trail name yet, you'll always be "Fleet" to us.

Anyway, this was our final night of the first week. Tomorrow, we'd reach civilization and take a one-day break, which we'd discovered was called a "Zero Day" because it was a day in which we would hike zero miles. I never thought the word "zero" would come to mean such great things to me, but by the time our five-week hike ended, "zero" was my favorite word.

That night, Smiley taught me how to hang a bear bag with two lines instead of one—foregoing the need for one big, perfect, bear-bag hanging branch.

This campground had plenty of trees, but none of them had any long, strong branches. Most of the branches were about as thick as my finger and could barely hold our bear bag right against the trunk, let alone six feet away.

The solution? Two trees, two lines. Loop one parachute cord around one trunk, fifteen feet up at the base of a small branch, loop the second cord around a trunk just as high up and about twenty feet away. Attach the bear bag to the two lines in the very center of the two trees, then hoist both lines until the bear bag is suspended in midair, ten feet off the ground.

Let's see a bear get *that*.

Smiley was such a genial, easy-going guy that he and Dash hit it off from the first moment. Smiley further endeared himself to me when, upon hearing about my foot troubles, he offered me a couple packs of foot glide, a powder to apply to the feet to stop friction. It was nice of him to try to help me out, but while apparently foot glide is great for *preventing* blisters, it didn't work so well—nothing seemed to—once the blisters were already there. Since Kenosha Pass, I'd been applying and re-applying Neosporin and bandages of all different kinds: blister band-aids, moleskin, corn pads. Nothing lasted for long, but I kept at it.

Still, it was awfully cool of Smiley to be concerned, and it was just another example of hikers being amazing, super helpful human beings.

The next day, Dash and I continued on. Down and up, down and up and finally, we stood at the edge of a precipice. In the valley below sprawled the beautiful sight of Breckenridge. Buildings and lodges and paved roads nestled between our ridge and Copper Mountain on the far side.

We had reached the end of our first week.

13

ZERO DAY

WHEN WE CRESTED that rise overlooking Breckenridge, a profound relief swept through me. We were almost there. The barely-imaginable thirty-three miles I'd contemplated while hobbling about at Kenosha Pass had been reduced to one series of switchbacks.

Of course, those switchbacks seemed to go down and down forever. Did I bite my lip and brace myself for the pain? Yes. Yes, I did.

Over the past two days, I'd become an expert on the best ways to avoid foot pain while I walked, to angle my feet such that the weight of body and pack pressed down on parts of my feet that weren't a blistered mess. Like the outer edges.

For this exercise in levitation, inclines were the best. Flats were okay. Downhill was agony. There was just no way to avoid my blisters when going downhill. My feet pushed into the front of the Cruel Shoes—which I'd jokingly taken to calling them based on an old Monty Python skit—forcing the pressure to land squarely on the ball of my foot, where the largest and rawest blisters were.

I took a deep breath as I stood there, watching Dash skip down the switchbacks. He was the opposite of me. He hated inclines. Flats were fun, a time to be chatty, and he loved declines. He looked over his shoulder at me as I watched him.

"We're almost there," he called up, already a full switchback down, which meant he was about fifty yards down the trail, but only about twenty feet below me. If I'd chosen to leap, I'd have landed on top of him. "You got this!" he encouraged.

I felt so proud of him. I'd started this journey being the cheerleader. Now he was. Not only that, but before we'd started out that morning, he'd offered to take almost everything out of my pack and put it in his. He took the tent, the stove, all of my extra food, and the chargers. He took pretty much everything except my clothes. The pack he now carried so effortlessly as he skipped down the trail was probably sixty-five pounds.

"I'm right behind you," I lied as he continued to increase his lead. "Just stop at the bottom, K?"

"You got it!" he yelled back, and continued cruising down.

I just kept repeating my mantra.

It's almost over. It's almost over. It's almost over.

The switchbacks went back and forth, back and forth. I winced with each step, and I dreamed about cheeseburgers and fries. I dreamed about a comfortable bed. I dreamed about just…stopping, not having to live my life in pain management. I dreamed about putting my feet up and not using them for a whole day.

Those dreams got me to the bottom of that mountain.

When I finally reached the point where the trail flattened out, I found Dash lying down, as if the packed dirt path were a bed. He lounged on his backpack, reading the Data Book.

"Come on. Let's find mom," I said. "Uppy uppy." I didn't want to walk anymore, and the sooner we reached Lara, the sooner that sweet fantasy would become a reality.

He hopped up and we started wending our way through the condo complexes toward Highway 9.

Despite my urgent desire to get to the rendezvous and begin power lounging, it felt strange heading into this land where everything was made by humans. I didn't realize just how accustomed to the wilderness I'd become until that moment. An awareness of things I hadn't had to pay attention to for a week—stoplights, cars, street directions, timetables—suddenly came back in a rush. I found my mind shifting from the trail mindset of "focusing on seven things" to the city mindset of "worrying about four hundred and eighty-two things."

After getting turned around a couple of times—if my feet hadn't hurt so much, I'd have laughed at how I could now navigate the wilderness, but I couldn't navigate a small town—we finally got going in the right direction. With a few phone calls to Lara, we agreed to meet at the intersection of the highway and Tiger Road, only a mile away from us.

It was the longest mile I'd hiked that week.

We finally met up with her after walking up a biking/jogging trail that ran alongside the highway. We threw our packs gratefully into the back of the minivan. I kissed Lara and told her how glad I was to see her, then I slumped into the passenger side of the car with a great big sigh.

Let me tell you about Zero Days. The name comes from an aspect of the trail that is important to every hiker on every single day: how many miles did you go?

"I had a twenty-mile day."

"I'm shooting for an eighteen-mile day today."

"Because of the weather, we decided to stop at a nine-mile day."

Zero Days are so called because you gain zero miles. They are a day of rest. Take a swim in a hot springs. Go get a massage. Eat in a restaurant. Or just lie about in a hotel room all…day…long.

As I sank back into that cushioned car seat, I also sank into the knowledge that I didn't have to worry anymore. I didn't have to think about falling off a cliff or running out of water, about hurting my feet or the weight of the pack cutting into my shoulders, whether my son was too far ahead or too far behind. I could just sit there, not lifting a finger to do anything.

Zero Days. Are. Amazing.

And boy, did I need one. I didn't realize just how blown out I was until I got into that seat. Lara kept looking over at me with a half-amused, half-concerned look as she drove us to an Airbnb downtown. We parked, dragged our stuff up to the room, then Dash and I reveled in taking our first showers in a week.

Afterward, Dash was amped up. His phone was charged. He could communicate with his friends, and he had no end of stories for them. Conversely, they told him how summer in Denver had been boring without him.

For my part, I finally got what I'd been wanting for four days. Freshly scrubbed and clean, with bandages on my feet, I fell onto the bed and put those suckers up in the air. I vowed not to move from that spot for twenty-four hours.

That night, we ordered cheeseburgers and Cokes from Empire Burgers. I did a build-it-myself burger with sautéed onions, mushrooms, cheese, and bacon. We also ate more fries than a half-dozen college kids with the munchies, including a gloriously decadent Empire menu special called "loaded fries," which had chili, cheese, and bacon too.

I must pause here in reverence, because I want you to hear me when I say this: if you're ever in Breckenridge, get a burger from Empire Burgers. It was the juiciest, cheesiest, mushroomiest, baconiest burger I've ever tasted. I ate until I had a stomachache. And then I ate some more. I experienced literal tingles throughout my body.

Not kidding. Best. Burger. Ever.

And that night, I actually slept. I recall nothing from the moment I put my head to the pillow to the moment sunlight speared through the crack in the drapes. I'm pretty sure Dash snored—the Airbnb Lara booked was a studio, so the bed was right there in the main room with the couch where Dash slept—but I didn't hear it. I slept like a felled log.

I awoke in the morning refreshed and happy to spend a leisurely day in bed. Dash woke up ready for the next adventure. He wanted to walk around Breckenridge and explore.

Me, I kept my promise. I tended my poor feet and kept them elevated. I ate food. I stayed in bed. Well, mostly.

During our brief meet-up at Kenosha Pass, I had asked Lara to bring a number of things with her to Breckenridge. First, of course, was extra food—above and beyond the assigned stashes I'd set aside at home for the next legs of the journey. The next item I'd requested was a noise-canceling headset. I just couldn't imagine being able to finish this entire trail on a couple hours of sleep a night. And I'd also asked her to bring my shoes. All of my shoes. Like, every pair of shoes I owned. I told myself that any one of my other pairs would be an improvement over the Cruel Shoes.

I was wrong.

While Dash and Lara explored Breck, I sorted through and tested each of my shoes, and not a single pair felt better than the Cruel Shoes. The damage had been done, and it didn't seem to matter what I put on my feet. One pair hit the blisters even worse. Another pair was so loose my foot slid all over. A third pair was too blown out. Pair after pair after pair, and not a single one could pamper the sore spots.

By the time I'd gone through all the pairs and put on the Cruel Shoes again, they actually felt the best of all of them.

Ugh.

I took a deep breath and told myself that this was just part of the trail. I'd wanted my feet to toughen up, and this was what that looked like. I decided to continue dancing with the Cruel Shoes.

God, I was an idiot. But I guess we all need to learn at our own pace.

While I was up, I also washed out the Platypus, then went through our packs. I swapped out our dirty clothes for clean ones and sorted the food stores for next week.

We had burgers again that night. I actually broke my vow

and limped down to Breckenridge Brewery with Lara and Dash.

And the world had changed.

Every person—every single person I saw—was wearing a mask. I felt like I'd been dropped in the middle of some sci-fi movie about a pandemic. When Dash and I had left Denver a week ago, the statewide mask mandate hadn't been issued yet, so when I'd walk down the streets, most people weren't wearing masks—maybe one in ten.

Now *everyone* wore them. When we'd hit the trail, I'd been hoping that by the time we got back to Denver, the whole COVID thing would have blown over.

I couldn't possibly have known that, in July of 2020, we had only seen the beginning of how COVID was going to change our lives. At the time, seeing everyone wearing masks just seemed chilling.

I did my best to turn my attention away from it and, that evening, I actually began to feel as optimistic as I could about my feet. They still hurt, but the day's rest had done wonders for them. I'd say the pain had been cut by about half.

But that night, as we returned from the restaurant and settled into the cozy condo, we ran into a completely different challenge.

"I don't think I want to spend my entire summer doing this," Dash said. "I mean, it's my whole summer! When we get back, I'll only have a week to play with my friends, and then I have to go back to school. And come on, a full week on The Colorado Trail, that's already pretty cool. We've already accomplished something here. I don't need to hike the whole thing."

His return to the posh luxuries of civilization had drawn him in and taken hold. He missed home, missed eating burgers whenever he wanted, missed connecting with other people on his phone, missed playing on his Xbox.

"I know it's a lot," I said.

"What is summer really for, Dad? It's to have fun."

"And you're not having fun anymore?"

He frowned. "It's just... It's not that. It's just that I don't know if I want to do this for four more weeks."

He'd been singing praises of the trail just yesterday. And I thought about the light in his eyes in Segment 4 when he'd said he wanted to finish the whole thing. That's when *I'd* committed. But as the father, I had to do more than just commit myself. I had to hold the fire for him. I not only had to make myself soldier on, but I had to remind him how he'd felt, the passion he'd had for this epic journey. I knew that the treasures at the end would be far greater than an extra few weeks lying around the house and playing Xbox. I had to nudge him past this moment.

"Okay," I said. "I feel what you're feeling. Believe me." I pointed at my feet. "I've got big reasons not to get back out there. But we made a pact—"

"I know," he interjected sullenly.

"We cannot quit until after the second week," I persisted. "Not you. Not me."

He didn't say anything, and I could almost see inside his mind, see him casting about, looking for some excuse that would circumvent the pact. Some really good, convincing reason he didn't have to keep going.

He didn't come up with one.

"We have to do at least one more week," I prompted at his silence.

"Yeah," he grunted, then turned away, stuck in his earphones and ignored me.

Okay, so this *is going to be a thing,* I thought.

My son is a passionate person, prone to jet off in one direction, then to turn on a dime and do something else. I'd predicted this moment, and I was exceedingly glad I'd prepared beforehand with our pact about the two weeks. But I knew I hadn't heard the last of this.

With Dash plugged into his phone and doing his best to ignore me, Lara and I finally had a chance to catch up. I told her stories from the trail—anything and everything aside from my ravaged feet. Even I was sick of that topic by now.

She told me about work. Things were not going well, and she was stressed out. At the end of the previous year there had been a change-up in leadership, and the office had gone from hopeful for the new direction, to confusion about what was expected, to downright fear of the wheels coming off the wagon. Now, every single employee thought they might get fired when they came into work each day. Nobody knew exactly what their roles were, let alone how to accomplish them to their highest ability. It was like everyone had taken a collective breath and was waiting for the axe to fall.

When she finished painting the picture, I lay back, stunned.

"God honey, that's awful," I said. I knew it had been a little dicey when I left, but it now sounded like things had gone from bad to worse.

"I don't know what else to do except keep doing my best," she said.

"You always do," I murmured, but I suddenly wondered if that was going to be enough. And if it wasn't, what did that mean for the family?

The uncomfortable truth, for me, is that though I write full time, I don't yet make enough money as an author to support our family. From 2003 through 2017, I had provided the bulk of our income through a nice little career in the non-profit sector, while Lara—as a certified massage therapist—had supplemented our income with massage clients. In 2016, when the kids were grown enough, she'd expressed interest in pursuing a new career outside of massage therapy. And she'd wanted more than the daily Herculean task of being mother and homemaker.

I'd been excited at the prospect of finally turning my attention to full-time writing and being the stay-at-home dad while she took on the nine-to-five role.

We'd phased me out of my day job over the course of two years and, as of January of 2017, we switched roles.

Throughout, I'd felt a low-grade guilt. Despite her constant support of my writing, despite her near-daily

ORDINARY MAGIC

affirmations that she believed in what I was doing, I still felt like I was letting her down. Every year that I didn't replace my previous income with what I made from writing, I felt like I was failing to hold up my end of the household, that I was following some pipe dream that could never be realized.

I constantly felt I needed to be earning more, and that if the novels weren't selling well enough, maybe the solution was to get back out there and get a day job to take the load off of her.

Now here I was out of the house, out of touch, spending weeks in the wilderness, and suddenly Lara's income was on shaky ground. If she lost her job, it could be catastrophic for us.

There was only one thing to do. If Lara was in trouble, it was "all hands on deck" to fix the problem. What the hell was I doing out here hiking through the wilderness when there were real issues to be handled?

"Okay, well..." I said, feeling a bite of disappointment mixed with a wash of relief. "We'll come back."

"No," she said immediately. "No, you won't."

"Honey, if we've got to prepare for a storm, I need to be at home."

"No, you need to be here." She gestured at Dash. "I can see a change in him already."

Dash was still sullen and oblivious, earbuds in, fingers working the touchscreen of his phone.

"You can?" I said playfully.

"Recent frustrations aside, you know what I'm saying. He was glowing when you got off the trail yesterday. Being in the wild makes him happy."

"You know he said he wanted to quit tonight."

She rolled her eyes. "Of course he did. He's gotten to reconnect with his friends, play on his phone, lie around this nice condo, eat junk food. This is easy. The trail is work."

"Yeah."

"This adventure is going to be with him for the rest of his life," she said. "And he gets to do it with you. I'm so glad you're in a place where you can take the time to do this." She touched my cheek. "I'm going to be fine. *We're* going to be fine. You concentrate on this. I'll handle the stuff at home."

I kissed her. Because when someone is so freakin' awesome, you have to kiss them.

I've said it before and I'll say it again. Lara is amazing. And despite what some may think, I didn't marry her *just* because she's drop-dead gorgeous. It's because of her indomitable will. She's a badass.

Don't believe me?

Try these two stories on for size. One's for fun, just to give you a glimpse. One's to make you a believer, like me.

So I've mentioned how strong my son is. He got that from Lara, not from me.

Don't get me wrong. I'm physically strong enough. But mine comes from being big—size does have advantages. Lara's physical strength comes from…I don't even know. She's a freak of nature. Her individual muscle strands are, like, radioactive or something. Pound for pound, she's ridiculously strong.

Okay, so let's flash back to the late nineties. Lara is living on Grand Cayman Island as a massage therapist. One day, at the height of her beach-body fitness, she is strolling alongside the ocean in a bikini and she sees a group of twenty-something boys having a pull-up contest. They're grunting and huffing and chinning-up on a stout, horizontal tree branch a short distance from the surf.

She walks over and says hello.

Now, Lara has never mastered the 'giggly ingénue' facade used by so many women in so many situations. She actually can't do it. I even tease her about it. I'll hear some pop chanteuse on the radio or see some starlet on the flatscreen give a Hollywood giggle, and I'll beg Lara to duplicate it. Sometimes she'll try for me. It's hilarious. She can never do it.

But on this day, she sees the pull-up enthusiasts and I envision her playing the ingénue to perfection.

So she grins and asks the young muscly boys what they're

doing—as if she doesn't know already—and they tell her.

"Who's winning?" she asks.

"Best is fifteen so far," says a proud shirtless man with swelling pecs and a washboard stomach.

"Wow," Lara says. "Do you mind if I…" She nods at the tree branch.

The shirtless man seems surprised, then grins. Smiles spread across the faces of his friends as well. "You want to do pull-ups?" he asks.

"I mean, I could try…" she says dubiously, cocking her head and looking up at the branch.

The boys take an eager step back, nodding heads and murmuring encouragement.

"Yeah, sure!"

"Do it up."

"Awesome."

They don't think she's serious. They think she's flirting, that she'll struggle through one pull up—maybe two—then laugh and drop to the ground, keep flirting, and maybe go for a drink.

Instead, she jumps up, sets her hands, and rips off twenty-five pull-ups. Then she drops to the sand and walks away without a word, leaving the young toughs behind, stunned.

My wife. Badass.

So yeah. Me. So in love with her. I mean, let's set aside the most obvious things she's done for our family—like bearing our two children, being the best mom on the planet, or bringing home the money that allows me to write full-time—she's just awesome in general. She's kind. She's thoughtful. Her first reaction is to look out for others. Her *first* reaction.

See, I have to remind myself to think of others. Call it a writer's professional self-absorption. Call it my truncated childhood, that lack of a safety net. Call it plain selfishness. Whatever you call it, I don't naturally think of others first. I have to work at it.

But Lara does it naturally. It impresses me day after day, and I revere her for it. Just standing next to her reminds me to strive to do better, to *be* better, to stay alert for how I can help.

Maybe she so often thinks about how to help others who are having difficulty because she's been through so much herself. I mean, I've mentioned some of my own traumas, but this woman has been through the grinder.

If there's such a thing as karma, she must have been a nefarious bastard in a previous life because nobody should have to deal with what she's gone through. Especially not someone so awesome.

So, again, all of these are reasons I love her, but I was telling you why I'd committed the rest of my life to her: her indomitable will. It was because, when I looked into her eyes, I knew she would never give up. Not on me. Not on my children. Not ever.

And it started with rock climbing.

When Lara was in her early twenties, just after graduating from The Colorado College where we met, she was a boss rock climber. It was something her older brother did pretty heavily, and that might have gotten her into the sport initially. Or it might have been because rock climbing was totally a Colorado College thing to do. I don't know.

By her senior year, the woman was leading 5.11 pitches which, if you know anything about rock climbing, is hard to do. On this particular day, she had just finished climbing with friends in Boulder Canyon and was cleaning the equipment at the top of the route. For those climbing novices out there, "cleaning" equipment means taking it off the route, packing it up, and heading out for the day.

As she was undoing the anchor, she tugged on a piece of webbing that was stuck. It came free and she stepped back to catch her balance. Except there wasn't a step there.

She said she remembered hearing screaming, but she doesn't remember if it was her, her friend who was standing right next to her on the cliff, or the people on the ground who saw her fall.

She plummeted eighty feet to the rocks below.

Eighty feet is the equivalent of an eight-story building. The next time you have the opportunity to look out an eight-story window or stand atop an eight-story building, imagine jumping. That's how far she fell.

Afterward there was great speculation as to how she managed to live. Was it that she'd landed just right, feet first, then knees, and crumpled into a perfect ball that saved her from breaking her back? Was it that she'd hit the only patch of dirt in that hard landscape of tumbledown boulders? Or was it that an angel had followed her down and given her that one-in-a-million chance to live?

Whichever it was, she came as close as a person ever comes to dying.

She broke every bone in her body except her back. Fractured skull. Pelvis in five pieces. Shattered right foot. Tibia. Fibula. Both femurs. Both arms.

She remembers nothing after that breathless moment when she stepped backward onto air. She doesn't remember the fall, doesn't remember the landing. She doesn't remember the rest of the entire day. But one of the volunteers from Rocky Mountain Rescue visited her in the hospital afterward. He filled in some of the blanks. He told her she had actually been conscious when they'd scooped her onto a body board.

"We're going to have to move you," he'd told her. She had crumpled into a ball at the base of a boulder, knees under her, leaning forward with her head against the rock.

"I know," Lara had said.

"It's going to hurt," the man had replied.

"It's okay," she'd said. "I know you have a job to do. Do your job. It's okay."

It makes me tear up just thinking about that. Broken at the bottom of the cliff, Lara was still trying to take care of people. *She* was trying to ease *his* worries.

They rushed her to Boulder Community Hospital, but even with all the modern medical technology at their fingertips, the doctors didn't expect her to live.

She proved them wrong.

After they stabilized her, after she came through multiple

surgeries and was finally out of the woods, she convalesced in the hospital for weeks. Soon, the doctors met with her again. They were elated she'd pulled through. That was the good news. But it was time to face the bad news. She wasn't going to walk again. There was just too much damage to the hips and legs. She was going to be in a wheelchair for the rest of her life.

Lara listened, but didn't comment. She didn't cry, didn't yell at them, didn't curse the heavens. She went back to focusing on healing her body.

And she proved them wrong a second time.

Months later, at Mapleton Rehab—with a pelvic fixator sticking out of her body—Lara took her first steps since the accident. Her mother said it was more emotionally moving than when Lara had taken her very first steps as a baby.

The doctors were stunned and happy, of course. So they waited a while before telling her the final two pieces of bad news.

"Your right foot was crushed," they said. "Yes, you managed a few steps on it, but it will never hold up over time. We took the shattered bones and just pushed them together as best we could. It's shaped roughly like a foot, but it's not a foot. It will deteriorate, you see? Probably sooner rather than later. It simply isn't going to be able to stand up to your weight, not for more than a step or two. It's going to have to be amputated."

She listened, then said, "What's the second piece of bad news?"

"You aren't going to be able to have babies."

When she didn't say anything, they continued. "It's your hips. They've been broken into so many pieces, there's just too much damage there. Most likely, you won't be able to conceive a child in the first place. But even if you do, you won't be able to carry the baby to full term."

"Okay," she said. And they left her alone.

She proved them wrong on all counts.

More than a decade later, she carried our daughter to full term and gave birth to her at home with a midwife and no interventions of any kind. Two and a half years after that, she gave birth to our son in the same way.

Moreover, she kept her right foot for eighteen years. She walked. She biked. She even went back to that cliff in Boulder Canyon and climbed it again. The woman would not be cowed.

And then, after eighteen years, she finally underwent the amputation voluntarily. When I asked her why, she said, "I think I'd like to take up taekwondo. You know, maybe get my black belt."

And that's exactly what she did.

She is my star. My inspiration. My wife.

And every time she is...well...so Lara-like, as she was in that dim condo that night as she encouraged me to continue with The Colorado Trail, I'm filled to the brim with gratitude.

"If you need me," I said to her after we'd finished kissing. "If you need me, you tell me. I'll come home."

"I know," she said.

"I love you," I said.

She winked. "This trip isn't just important for Dash, you know. It's important for you, too. It reminds you that you're an adventurer."

Her simple statement struck me. She hadn't said, "you *were* an adventurer," but rather "you *are* an adventurer," like it was something intrinsic, like it was something that never goes away. Like it was something I'd forgotten.

"Hey," I said softly. "Thank you. Thank you for everything. For driving out here, for bringing us food, for taking care of us at Kenosha Pass. For everything."

She kissed me again. "You're doing a good thing here," she said. "You take care of your part. I'll take care of mine."

Indomitable.

14

COPPER MOUNTAIN

THE NEXT DAY, Lara dropped us off at the Segment 7 trailhead. She kissed us, hugged us, took pictures, and drove away.

The next leg of our journey was over a hundred miles—the longest stretch we would hike without a break. After our gloriously decadent Zero Day, it was a rough mental re-entry for me. I'd slept through the night in a comfortable bed, given my poor feet a rest, and remembered just how much easier everything was in the arms of civilization. The idea of hiking on blistered feet and grabbing only three hours of sleep a night over the next hundred miles was daunting. I admit my heart ached a little as the mini-van vanished around the corner.

Then Lara was gone, and any alternative choices went with her. We were on our own again, me and Dash and the items in our packs versus the Rocky Mountains. My feet, though not fully healed, felt much better. I had determined they'd continue healing, that the next seven days weren't going to be consumed with pain management.

"Let's get to it," I said, and started up the trail.

Dash didn't say anything. He wasn't happy at being denied a return to Denver, and I kept quiet to give him mental space.

Segment 7 took us out of Breckenridge and practically straight up. It was three-and-a-half thousand feet of elevation gain over nine miles to get to the top of Copper Mountain.

With Dash's hatred of inclines, this constant "up" did not improve his mood.

He stomped ahead of me, knowing I couldn't keep pace with him, but after about forty-five minutes, he drifted back to walk next to me. Apparently, he'd finally figured out something to say. I imagined he'd been spending his time coming up with the right approach to berate/guilt/convince me that we should turn around and give up the trail.

Of course, I'd been spending an equal amount of time expecting—and preparing for—this attempt. Two can play at that game.

"You're kind of forcing me to do this," he accused.

"I'm totally forcing you to do this," I said breezily.

He pressed his lips into a line.

When he didn't respond, I kept a deliberately upbeat tone and said, "Hey, we agreed to do the first two weeks. You're stuck for it. I'm stuck for it. It's easy to quit in the first week. Everything's new and frustrating. Painful. And there's so much distance to go. So we can't give ourselves that out. We have to do at least two weeks. After that, it's your choice."

"And when we get to Buena Vista, you're going to force me to do the third week," he said.

"Nope," I told him.

He shook his head. "You say that now. But you're going to guilt me into it once we get there."

I could see the set up. One thing about having smart children is that they know how to work you. Dash was drawing me out. He was coming at me during a moment where he hoped my attention was elsewhere—the shining sun, thoughts of the trail, my blistered feet—anywhere other than a week from today. He was hoping to draw out a promise. In Breckenridge, he hadn't fought me about continuing because he knew he didn't have a leg to stand on. We'd made a pact. So he'd backed down, albeit reluctantly.

But if he could extract a promise from me right now, *he'd* be the one on solid ground a week from now, not me. That way, when he brought this up again when we got to Buena Vista—our next planned Zero Day—*I'd* have to back down.

But I had a plan.

I mean, of *course* I wanted to force him to continue after Buena Vista. I had enough skin in the game at this point that I wanted to finish the trail for my own personal reasons. I wanted those four-hundred-and-eighty-five miles. I wanted to be able to say I'd done it.

And by the time we hiked into Buena Vista, we would be less than *thirty-five miles* from the midpoint. We'd be more conditioned, more knowledgeable. And I assumed my feet would be fully healed.

In short, the third week would be easier in every way. We would have almost broken the back of the beast. And if we could hike through that third week—if we could just get past that week—there was no way Dash would quit. We'd be too close to the end.

Obviously, my challenges on the trail were going to be physical. Dash's were going to be mental, and more important than mine by far. Physical pain comes and goes. But how Dash handled this moment of hardship might set an example for how he handled hardship for the rest of his life.

We'd had a moment like this once before, and it had also been on a mountain. When Dash was eleven, he and I had hiked Mount Bierstadt together, his first 14'er—which is hiker slang for a mountain taller than fourteen thousand feet.

It went like this:

We climbed up and up all morning and, when we were just five hundred feet from the top, he wanted to quit. He had a headache. He hated the hiking. This whole 14'er thing "sucked." He was barely shuffling along and looked absolutely miserable, so I reluctantly relented.

The moment I did, he whooped and skipped down the

trail.

When I saw how much energy he had left, my whole perspective shifted. It was like he'd been putting on an act for me. So I stopped him, made him turn around, and forced him to continue hiking upward to the summit—over much complaining.

My reasoning was that if I forced him to continue, he'd know the difference between stopping shy of a goal and pushing through to the end. I wanted him to understand that five hundred feet—a mere thirty minutes of gutting it out—could be the difference between success and failure. I wanted him to feel it for himself, the accomplishment. If we stopped short, I feared it would affect how he approached his next goal. It could possibly even affect his confidence. "Oh, I'm just the guy who *almost* hiked a 14'er."

Alternatively, reaching the goal despite the hardship would bring a multitude of advantages. A taste of victory. Confidence in his abilities. Experience.

And bragging rights, of course. He'd be able to tell everyone that he'd climbed his first 14'er when he was eleven.

So yeah. I had turned him around, made him go back up, and we'd summited Mt. Bierstadt. Afterward, as we descended the slope, his headache developed into a migraine that lasted for the rest of the trail and an hour beyond. He puked in the car on the way home and was miserable.

I felt horrible.

The whole ride home and forever after, I'd been uncertain if I'd made the right call. I really couldn't say if it was a bad dad moment, or a good one.

But I can say this. The nausea faded. The headache faded.

And Dash still tells people he climbed his first 14'er at age eleven.

So now, as Dash maneuvered me into a corner to extract a promise that would set him free in Buena Vista after only two weeks on the trail, I relived the Mt. Bierstadt lesson. I considered doing to him in Buena Vista exactly what I'd done to him then. I mean, shouldn't I? Shouldn't I push him to continue for his own good? In the long term, he'd reaped nothing but benefits from summiting Bierstadt. All the bad stuff had faded and the good stuff had stayed.

And yet...this was different. He was older. He wasn't just some little kid who didn't know his capabilities. He was a teenager. It wasn't as important to show him what he could do. He was aware of his physical capabilities. At this stage, it seemed more important for *him* to push himself, to find his own grit, rather having me push him.

He had to make his own decision.

I didn't want Dash quitting the CT. Not now and not a week from now. But there was more at stake. He had to *want* to continue. The teenage years were his time to learn to make decisions and stand by them, to reap the benefits or pay the price of his choices without blaming—or crediting—me.

If I shamed, guilted, or cleverly maneuvered him into continuing after Buena Vista, the remainder of the trail would be like this. Him blaming me for making him do it. Him getting angry at me when something didn't go right instead of shouldering the responsibility for himself.

I wanted him to *choose* to excel, otherwise what's the point? Even if he did get into the habit of succeeding because I forced him at all the right moments, his victories would always come with the specter of his pushy father floating over his shoulder.

"Dash," I said after a long moment letting all of this run through my mind. "I'm not going to force you past the second week."

"Sure you aren't." He said it with zero confidence.

"Nope. I promise you right here and now. If you don't want to continue on after the second week, I'm not going to pressure you. I won't shame you. I won't guilt you. I won't try to manipulate you. It's going to be your decision. All yours."

He heard the sincerity in my voice, looked over his shoulder and caught my gaze.

"I'm serious," I said. "You've done a great job so far. It's like you were born for this. And I'll be honest with you. Do I think it would be a tragedy if you didn't finish? Yes. I do. But

I'm not going to make you. I may continue on my own." I winked. "But I won't force you to finish. We made a pact to go through the first two weeks. That's what you're on the hook for. Nothing more if you don't want it."

I could tell by his look that he believed me. He nodded, smiled, and all his frustration melted away. He started hiking with a spring in his step, and we chatted about fun stuff. Sophomoric jokes flew back and forth between us. We discussed Marvel movies and had "quote wars"—where we flung out an unattributed quote to see if the other person could guess the character and the movie.

We were back to the equilibrium we'd struck during the first week.

The hike up Copper Mountain was the toughest we'd hit so far. My feet were better, and it was mostly an incline, which they loved. But I still had to walk gingerly on the flats and mostly-flats. I would look ahead and plan my steps on pointy rocks, trying to put my weight on the arch of my foot and stay off the ravaged ball, where the blisters were. It actually worked. Unless I missed. Then it hurt like hell.

As we approached the summit, there were no trees. We could see the whole of Breckenridge behind us like a miniature model with little buildings, roads, and tiny cars. But the city seemed a barely significant patch of humanity when taken in with the giant mountains behind it. The slopes were a dozen shades of green intermingled with browns and blacks, and sometimes the shadows of clouds would darken everything like spots on a dairy cow.

I kept looking at the vista as I walked. After I'd had my fill of the majestic view, I focused only on the trail. There were interesting formations right in front of me, fascinating veins of tumbledown rock that had cascaded over—and become a part of—the trail. I took several pictures of their jagged jigsaw nature. It was almost as though, at the point where they crossed the path, a trail builder had assembled them into cobblestone patios. Heck, maybe they had!

The wind got crazy as we approached the summit. I'm not

sure if it blew harder because we were closer to the top, or if it just seemed that way because there were no trees to create a wind break.

Whatever, it was cold and windy when we topped the ridge at about one-thirty in the afternoon. Again, the Universe seemed to be watching over us. There were heavy gray clouds all around, patches of blue sky in between, and some sheets of rain in the distance, but we reached the top with no weather issues aside from that freezing wind. And in the middle of the afternoon. I began to wonder if the conventional wisdom about the dangers of afternoon thunderstorms was exaggerated. That was twice now we'd summited a peak later in the day, and we'd had no problems.

Dash, who'd complained prodigiously about the never-ending incline up Copper Mountain, seemed to throw off all discomfort. He didn't seem to feel the wind as we stood on the top. He just gazed toward the west at the layers upon layers of mountains in the distance. It was like we could see the whole of the Rockies.

I clapped him on the back and said, "Let's find a good place to take a picture. Then it's all downhill from here."

"Until the next mountain," he said.

"Until the next mountain," I echoed.

As we walked away, I looked back over my shoulder at the heavy gray clouds behind us, the patches of rain falling far away. I looked forward and saw the edge of the tree line far below. It'd only take us half an hour to get there. No problem.

We ran into Smiley on the other side of the ridge, and he offered to take pictures of Dash and me. We heartily accepted and chose a spot a few dozen yards away from the summit because there was a great sign posted. It read:

WARNING
YOU CAN DIE

Dash and I laughed and stood before the sign.

"I like that the Universe puts these little signs here for us, reminders of our mortality," I said. "Carpe Diem."

"Like She came out here with a pot of paint and a brush?" Dash gave me a sidelong look. "Painted this for us?"

"Who else?"

"Uh, the resort." He pointed to a line of smaller words on the sign:

You are leaving the ski resort
This is your decision point

"For skiers," he said. "Or snowmobilers."

Of course he was right. The sign had been made for the winter months, establishing the boundary of the resort for skiers, reminding anyone who went beyond this point that they might fall down the steep, snowy slopes or start an avalanche. Or both.

As Smiley got ready to take our picture, Dash and I stood behind the sign. I grinned and pointed down at the words as Smiley took pictures.

Dash glanced at the angle of my finger and let out an exasperated sigh. "Point at the sign right, Dad. Jeez. It looks like you're pointing at your junk."

I laughed and adjusted the angle of my finger.

We continued joking, bantering back and forth. The day was perfect. We were in good company and we had a spectacular view. I thought again that only those who hiked The Colorado Trail got to see this view. My mind was far away and filled with joy.

I had no idea that in less than twenty-four hours, Dash and I would see how fast joy could turn to fear in the wild. We were about to experience how quickly my arrogance could kill us.

And I'd look back at this moment and wonder if the Universe actually *was* sending us a warning.

15

LIGHTNING ON SEARLE PASS

AFTER COPPER MOUNTAIN, we finished our miles for the day on a nonstop decline. Ouch. We hiked past Copper Mountain Resort underneath the towering poles, cables, and chair lifts, above the quiet condos and the empty restaurants below. Shortly after we got clear of the resort, we witnessed the summer aftermath of several avalanches. Thousands of hundred-foot-tall dead pines had been snapped like twigs and thrown down the slope below the trail, scattered like sticks, like they weighed nothing. The tonnage of those trees, tossed so casually about, stunned me. It covered the slope like a giant's itchy blanket, trunks poking out every which way, a chaotic pattern that drew the eye.

Sawdust scattered the muddy ground where a few of the trees had fallen over the trail. They'd been chainsawed away, cutting a four-foot-wide path through so the trail could continue.

We spent that night just past Tenmile Creek, close to a development of some kind. It felt odd to unfurl our tent so close to those earth movers and the mobile homes that served as the construction office. The freshly turned and flattened earth was only a hundred yards away, and it looked like a giant parking lot with all of the cars and trucks of the construction workers sitting there. I felt exposed, and it again reminded me how comfortable I'd become with the deep woods, far away from things like cars and people.

That night, just before sunset, another hiker arrived at our campsite, politely asking if we minded if he put down stakes near us. We welcomed him warmly, and I again felt that safety-in-numbers feeling.

The man's name was Mark, and as we cooked up our respective dinners on our respective JetBoils, we talked. He'd hiked just about everything there was to hike. The Appalachian Trail, the Pacific Crest Trail, the John Muir trail. He also had a Platypus gravity water filter like we did, and he swore by it. He said he preferred it to any other kind of filtration system. It's all he used when he was on the trail.

Mark said he'd hiked twenty-eight miles that day, and the guy had to be north of sixty years old. Dash and I were both stunned, and Dash decided to make tomorrow our first twenty-mile day.

Mark passed on other bits of hiking wisdom to us, like reversing the bags when the Platypus flow began to slow down over time as the filter got full. "Put the clean bag high up, and the dirty bag down below. Let the clean water flow backward for a while. It cleans the filter."

He also pointed out that, for his old bones, carrying a lightweight chair was a beautiful luxury in camp. He popped that thing open before he even set up his tent, and I was instantly jealous.

His last bit of advice came as Dash went back to get something from our tent. Mark looked up from his cup of tea and said, "Your foot troubles are going to be fine. I've had more blisters and lost more toenails." He shook his head. "It's just part of the trail. We all go through it. And the key to making it easier, especially in the morning... Ibuprofen." He smiled as he said it.

I laughed, and took the advice to heart that very night.

I think it was safe to say that Dash and I liked Mark immediately.

The next morning, we awoke to find Mark already packed and gone. As I mentioned before, early rising and quick packing was not our strong suit. Mark probably had his boots beating the trail by five-thirty in the morning, whereas Dash and I didn't get underway until two hours later.

I had awoken with great optimism about my feet. They actually felt better than the previous day, and I was hopeful that I was finally on the mend. That day, as we got underway, my hiking speed picked up to the point that I could almost keep up with Dash. On the inclines, I matched him. But on the declines and straight-aways, he still left me in the dust.

It was about noon when we started hiking up the next mountain toward Searle Pass. Once again, the sky was gorgeous and the vistas were breathtaking. I loved how the broken grays of the sullen clouds mixed with the blue sky, and then with the purple-and-green mountain horizon.

We summited Searle Pass at twelve forty-five in the afternoon and took a bunch of photos. It had been a hard climb. Not quite as hard as Copper Mountain, but we were definitely feeling it. Thankfully, according to the Data Book, our next water source was only a mile past the summit.

By the time we got to it, I was looking forward to changing out my socks—a foot-saving habit I'd adopted since Breckenridge. I'd learned the hard way that sweaty feet create blisters just as fast as getting drenched in a rainstorm. So every time I felt even a little slippage in my boots, I'd stop and swap out socks. Two spare pairs fluttered out behind me always, attached by bungee cords to the back of my pack so they could hang in the sun. With this method, I always had a dry pair.

We plopped down next to the river—which was right where the Data Book said it would be. I took off my boots, stripped off my socks, and put my feet into my comfy Crocs.

Ahhhh...

As I went about doing my sock switcharoo, Dash tried his

hand at setting up the water filter by himself. He was funning around, acting like a giant squirrel, holding the dirty water bag up against his chest. At twelve thousand feet, we were above tree line, so there were no branches around to hang it on. So Dash became our "tree," allowing gravity to do its thing, directing the flow of water. I took a goofy picture of his smile and that pose—

Thunder cracked overhead. It was so loud, so close, that it felt like someone had thumped a fist against my chest.

"Jesus!" I jumped. Icy pins prickled up the back of my neck.

"That's not good," Dash said, his eyes wide. He'd flinched into a crouch and almost dropped the bag.

We both swiveled. The sky was blue overhead, as it had been the whole morning, but right behind us the clouds bunched dark and ugly behind the saddle of Searle Pass. We'd been standing right there only half an hour ago—right where the lightning had just struck. A mile away.

Oh shit, I thought.

On the top of Copper Mountain, the moment we'd gone over the ridge, the trail had dropped steeply. We'd reached the tree line less than thirty minutes after we'd summited.

Now, I swiveled my head and looked down the trail ahead of us, hoping it would be the same—a quick dash down the slope and into the trees.

It wasn't.

The trail ran alongside the ridge, bald and exposed to the sky. It went on as far as I could see. There were no trees. The closest forest was a mile below us, down a treacherously steep decline that could easily trap us at the edge of a drop-off.

Above tree line, a person is the tallest thing around. The next tallest things around are marmots. Want to bet who's more likely to get struck by lightning? I'll give you a hint: marmots are shorter than a cinderblock. And there are about a million of them bouncing happily around above tree line.

Hikers, on the other hand, are relative lightning rods, chock full of lightning-conducting water, and carrying materials like metal hiking poles, pots, tent poles, spoons, shovels, cups and such. So you don't want to be in a lightning storm on a peak. Everybody knows that.

Thunder boomed again, and we both flinched.

"Dad, I'm scared. What do we do?" Dash said. I could hear the panic in his voice.

My mind raced. There was no cover. The fastest way to tree line was back the way we'd come, but that would mean running into the teeth of the storm. The black clouds bunched behind Searle Pass like they were eager to tumble over, eager to get to us.

I glanced up at the little patch of blue directly overhead.

"Dad, what do we do?" Dash repeated.

I'd been in enough crunches to know that, in a situation where all the options sucked, the worst option was to lose your ability to think. To waste time and mental energy on things that didn't matter.

I wanted to berate myself for putting us in this situation. If I'd been in my city mind, I would have. It was shockingly clear I'd made a string of stupid mistakes and gotten away with them. Only this time, I hadn't. I'd ambled along, enjoying the sun and the fresh air and the gorgeous vistas, and I'd ignored the caution of summiting peaks in the afternoon.

All very well and good if we only had a half-an-hour sprint to reach the tree line, but there was no tree line in sight. Not along the trail. If I'd studied the Data Book to get the lay of the land, I'd have known that.

I'd surrendered all of my advantages. Now we were in the soup.

Well, working myself into hysterics would only lead to more stupid mistakes, like running back to Searle Pass to try to get back to the tree line. Or like careening headlong down an uncharted slope with no knowledge of what we might run into.

"First of all, we don't panic," I said calmly, even though my heart was hammering.

Thunder boomed again, louder, closer. We both ducked our heads like someone had thrown a rock at us.

"I AM panicking!" Dash said.

"We get off this ridge," I said as I stuffed the water filtration equipment into my pack. "We do what we need to do and we do it fast. You go first. Go now. Don't wait for me." I wanted him to get away from here. The storm was behind us, and we still had blue sky above. If he moved quickly, he might stay ahead of the storm. It might make that crucial difference when the lightning came. And he couldn't wait for me. I still had to put my boots on.

Another thunderclap rocked us.

"Go, Dash," I demanded. I stuffed the coils of the Platypus in my pack, clipped my Crocs onto the back. "I'll catch up."

"No," he said.

"Dash, you go!" I barked, shoving my feet into my socks.

"I'm not leaving you!" he barked back.

Damned stubborn kid! The dad in me got angry that he wouldn't just do what I told him, but I was also proud as hell. The kid wasn't going to leave my side. No matter what. Heroic little bastard.

A part of me—the part that was a scared little boy itself— was relieved. It wasn't a logical relief. There was no safety in numbers against lightning, but I felt it nonetheless as I shoved my feet into my boots and laced them up tight.

"Okay then," I said evenly. We were in this together. No matter what.

"Where do we go?" he asked as I capped my water bottles and stuffed them in their pouches. Thunder boomed again, so loud it hurt my ears. Cold sweat broke out on my scalp. Great. One more conductive substance, right on top of my head.

Thunder boomed again, and Dash hunched low, wincing over at the clouds that had started to come over the ridge. I spared an excruciating moment to double-check the site, to make sure we hadn't left anything behind. If I did something stupid in these hurried seconds—like panicking and running off without a piece of the Platypus, we'd end up in just as much trouble down the line. Ninety percent of what we carried was absolutely essential.

I saw nothing on the ground, nothing by the stream. We were good to go.

I hefted my pack onto my shoulders and we started running, making for that patch of sunlight that was no longer over our heads, but just up the trail. A light in the darkness.

As Dash pelted down the trail ahead of me, I looked to my right. The storm had come over the ridge at last, and for the first time I saw the lightning. It lanced down, a pearly branch striking the ridge no more than a football field away.

BOOM!

The thunder shook the ground. Thankfully, Dash didn't see the lightning strike, and I didn't tell him. That had been close. So close that the next one could be right on top of us.

We ran our asses off. Every step was painful. Flats weren't great for my feet even when I could concentrate on exactly how I placed them. It was torture to pound on them in a willy-nilly sprint with fifty pounds on my back. But when you're in the soup, you do what you have to do.

A marmot darted out ahead of us as the thunder cracked, driven by the storm. We'd seen a lot of the little guys above tree line, and they're usually chill. But this guy was as panicked as we were. He darted like he was being chased by a lion, his little tail spinning like a propeller.

I thought about how I might reassure Dash somehow. I mean, we could get hit by lightning at any second, but being terrified wasn't going to help him.

I yelled over the wind to him.

"As long as we stay under that blue sky, we'll be good!" I lied. The truth, of course, was that lightning can reach a long, long way. We weren't much safer underneath that blue with the storm so close, but I hoped it would give him something to focus on besides being terrified.

"And don't get close to the posts," I yelled. There were tall posts every now and then with the little tin signs bearing the Colorado Trail logo. I honestly had no idea whether lightning preferred the posts to a running human being, but I figured it was one more thing he could focus on instead of fear.

As I ran, I remembered a story about Lara's brother, the one who'd inspired her to become a rock climber. He was an avid outdoorsman and, in his youth, he'd been struck by lightning hiking a 14'er right here in Colorado. He'd said the lightning hit him out of the clear, blue sky. The blast literally blew him out of his boots. Miraculously, he survived, but I remember him telling me that the metal knob on top of his ball cap had burned a little circle on his scalp.

I was wearing a ball cap with a little metal knob on top.

Irrationally, I swiped my ball cap off my head and held it in my hand as I pounded after Dash.

Running from lightning is nerve-wracking. I don't recommend it. It's not just because I was afraid we might die. It's because it was impossible to know if we were even helping the situation by doing what we were doing. I mean, maybe the smart thing to do would be to just lie down in the wide-open field and become as flat as possible, rather than running upright and presenting a target.

It's not like running from a bull, for example. I mean, you can see the bull. You can hear its snorts, the pounding of its hooves. You know when it's close.

Lightning isn't like that. It's either going to strike—and you're dead—or it's not, and you're fine. There's no warning beforehand so that maybe you can throw yourself to the side at the last second. Lightning only alerts you *after* it has come and gone. Who set up that crappy system anyway? By the time the thunder cracks, you're dead. Thunder isn't a warning. It's a victory cry.

But we kept at it. What else could we do? We had one advantage: the wind seemed to be blowing in our faces, which meant it was holding the storm back. And soon—bless that wind—we reached our sunny patch of sky. Under the sun, we ran flat-out for a mile, our fifty-pound packs bobbing up and slamming down on us.

I kept hoping we'd come around a bend, top a rise, and see that blessed tree line in our future. But after a mile of that flat, exposed trail, I began to despair.

Finally, we reached our limit and, gasping, we slowed to a walk for a moment while the storm gathered behind us.

"There's..." I huffed, "No downhill..." I yanked the Data Book from its pouch on my belt and flipped it open. Downhill was what we needed. Downhill would take us to the tree line.

Thunder boomed again, and I flinched. We were losing the distance we'd fought so hard to gain, but I had to check the book. I had to know when this damned trail started back down. How far before we'd be safe? Half a mile? Another full mile? How much longer would we have to run?

I scanned the book, and my heart fell. There was no down. We had to go up.

Around the next bend wasn't our salvation, it was a hike straight up to Elk Ridge, which was even higher than Searle Pass. Then, and only then, did the trail start on a two-mile downhill trek to the tree line.

That. Sucked.

"What's wrong?" Dash must have seen the look on my face. I quickly wiped it away and forced a smile.

"We gotta go up," I said.

"What?" he exclaimed.

"Elk Ridge is the high point, then the trail heads back down into the tree line."

He was shaking his head, scared. "I don't want to go up."

"I don't either. But it's either that or wait for the storm."

He looked dubious.

"It'll be all right," I said. "One more mile."

"A mile!"

"There's nothing else we can do. We just push as hard as we can. We stay with that blue sky. We get up and over as quick as we can and then we get the hell down."

He hesitated, then nodded. "Okay."

We began running again, and I was heartsick at what I'd done.

Of course, I *was* paying for it. All the running had made mincemeat of my feet. I hadn't dared stop to change my socks, and my feet were sliding, slamming into the sides of my shoes with every step, and each impact felt like an ice pick. I tried to ignore the pain as thunder cracked and lightning struck behind us, but I wondered if I'd reach a point where I just couldn't run anymore.

The switchbacks up to Elk Ridge were brutal. It was nearly straight up. We huffed and sweated in the diminishing sun. Back and forth and back and forth up tight switchbacks which weren't taking us any further away from the storm, only up. It seemed like we were stuck in the same place, just a few feet higher every time, while the storm closed in.

Higher… Up to an even more exposed point.

But the sun still shone on those dusty, rocky switchbacks while we sweated and pushed our shaky legs to keep going. Our luck held as the winds worked for us, holding the storm back, keeping that dark shadow poised over the places we'd been only minutes ago.

We kept our heads low as we crested Elk Ridge, shuffling like apes. A part of me wanted to stop and take a picture of that moment, of us atop the ridge, of the ugly storm behind us, maybe catch a lightning strike in the distance to remember this terrifying moment.

I didn't.

I decided not to tempt fate. Instead of taking a picture, I made a promise to the Universe instead.

Let us live, and I swear I'll never hike another summit between noon and three. Just please make this okay and I promise I promise I promise…

On the other side of the ridge, the trail dropped steeply, and I breathed an inward sigh of relief. We were still exposed, but we were off the highest point and Elk Ridge was now between us and the storm. We were no longer hiking *into* the danger zone. We were hiking away from it. Every step would take us closer to relative safety.

I staggered behind Dash, and he kept looking over his shoulder at me impatiently. The trail sagged like a long clothesline, leading to the saddle of Kokomo Pass. But when we were only halfway down that slope, I gasped in pain and stopped running.

"Dash, I have to stop. I have to change socks."

He frowned, looking back at the storm that was now bunching behind Elk Ridge like it had bunched behind Searle Pass. "Dad…"

"I'm sorry, buddy. I can't go any further. I gotta change out my socks. You go on ahead."

He rolled his eyes as if to say, "Not this again…" and put his hands on his hips. "Okay. We stop. Just do it quick."

I changed my socks in record time and popped two ibuprofen to cut the pain.

It made all the difference. My feet weren't slipping anymore, and with as fast as my heart was beating, those ibuprofen went straight to my brain. I felt like a new man.

We got down, over the saddle of Kokomo Pass, and dropped into a wide-open wildflower field before a distant horizon of pines. The storm, like an orc cracking a whip at our back, continued to boom. It had finally come up and over Elk Ridge and resumed its race to catch us. Though I was tired and in pain, I knew this wide-open field wasn't much better than an exposed ridge. It might even be worse. And we only had a quarter of a mile to go before the trees.

"Let's sprint," I huffed to Dash. "Let's put this field behind us."

He nodded, and we put in a last big push, sprinting the thousand feet into the trees.

The blue sky was completely gone by the time we made it to the tree line. The low heavy storm hovered over us now, but I felt like a weight had lifted. I thanked the Universe over and over in my mind, and I swore that I'd never do something so careless again.

I'd lucked out. I hadn't killed my son. And I imagined the Universe winking at me, as if to say, "That's your last mulligan. You're welcome." She'd given us three strikes. We'd summited Georgia Pass in the afternoon, and I'd contemplated the storms in the distance. We'd summited Copper Mountain in the afternoon, with the winds whipping about, storms in the distance. But I'd discounted the danger that had been so close until Searle Pass had lit up with lightning and thunder.

I'd gotten the message now. I may have a thick skull, but I do eventually learn. I was going to listen to the warning this time.

And I was going to read the hell out of that Data Book. No more of this "it'll all work out" shit. I was going to study our route and know what we were heading into.

Our new lease on life gave us quite a boost, and as the fear of our harrowing flight faded, I noted a positive after-effect: Dash and I had covered a phenomenal amount of ground in just a couple of hours.

It was just after three o'clock, and we'd already gone nearly fourteen miles for the day. This meant we could find a campsite with plenty of daylight left even if we pushed another six miles. We were amped. We were ready to do it, so we pushed on...

...for about three more miles, when we ran into Mark again. He had set up camp right by the trail, and we stopped to chat. We told him about our lightning experience, which was quickly fading from terror to tale. Mark nodded sagely.

"Yeah. You usually only have to do that one once," he said. "But if you ever get caught in a lightning storm again, just sit down."

"Sit down?" I asked incredulously.

"Yep. Sit down. Make yourself as low as you can. Wait it out."

I felt dubious. Thinking back, I couldn't imagine doing that. I mean, it would lower our profile to sit, but by and large, we'd still be about as tall as anything around.

"What about lying down?" I asked, thinking that if low was good, flat against the ground had to be better.

"Nope, don't do that. You want as little contact with the ground as possible. That's why you sit. On the balls of your feet if you can. Reduce your contact with the ground. Lying down gives you lots of touch points. You don't want that."

I smiled and thought, I'm never going to need that 'cause I'm never putting myself in that position again.

I was grateful that we were gone gone gone from that stupid storm. I just don't know if I could have huddled down, inactive, as lightning struck all around me and my son. I just don't know if I could have done that.

"Well," I said. "Dash and I made fantastic time when we were running. The upside is that I think we can bag our first twenty-mile day today."

"Ah," Mark said. "Well, I don't want to stand in the way of a young man's goal. Your first twenty-miler is a big one, but before you head on, I'd like to show you something."

"Oh?"

"Found a campsite that may be the best campsite on the entire CT. It's a sweet, hidden little spot. Not many people find it, I imagine. I'd have camped there myself, but I was already set up when I went exploring. If you're interested, I'll show it to you."

I was warmed by his generosity and his interest in giving something nice to us. I looked at Dash. He looked dubious. His heart was set on that twenty miles.

"Take you two minutes to look at it," Mark said. "Then you can decide."

Dash relented and Mark guided us down the slope to a hidden trail, barely more pronounced than a deer trail, and we went deeper into the woods. It opened up to a breathtaking vista at the top of Cataract Falls. Just beyond a flat little campsite, the world opened up into a panorama of forests and mountains. The creek leapt over the precipice, casting water thousands of feet down, much of it turning into mist on the way.

An old log structure—somewhere between a lean-to and a small cabin—perched at the edge of that cliff, and I tried to determine its purpose. It was too leaky to serve as a good shelter and too involved to have been the pet project of some thru-hiker.

I wouldn't come up with a good answer to this question

until the next day, when we would hike by Camp Hale, only four miles ahead on the trail. That's when I would decide the log lean-to had to be the summer project of a group of youthful campers who, perhaps, hiked up here to spend a night or two.

After seeing the unique majesty of the campsite, Dash allowed himself to be talked into staying, and he relinquished his twenty-mile goal for the day. We pitched our tent and had a nice relaxed dinner with Mark. With the creek gurgling in the background and the sun setting over that gorgeous vista, we listened to Mark's many stories and even told a few of our own.

As I lay down in the tent that night, I iced my feet against the drom, which was full of chilly river water, and I snuggled my upper body into my sleeping bag. Dash and I played with the noise-cancelling headset Lara had brought me in Breckenridge which had, unfortunately, been a bust. It simply had not been enough to shut out Dash's snoring. And on top of that, the thing was so thick that it woke me up every time I tried to roll over. So it had become a thirty-eight-dollar, half-pound dead weight dangling off the back of my pack.

But it gained renewed value that night as we messed around with it. Dash put it over his ears, and I said a string of rhyming words. He'd try to hear them and parrot them back accurately. The mistakes had us belly laughing. We switched back and forth until the game went stale, then settled down to get some rest.

Dash conked out in an instant, and the chainsaw snoring began. I lay there, smiling. There was something inevitable about his snoring now. We were on the trail. There were mountains. There was sunshine and rain. There were trees and summits and rocks. And there was Dash's snoring.

In some ridiculous way, I had come to count on it. It was…comforting, and that amused the hell out of me.

I fell to thinking about the day, and I could barely believe what we'd been through. We'd started out blissful and ignorant, had shifted into a high-adrenaline sprint for our lives, then shifted back to blissful again, though hopefully less ignorant. Now we were safely ensconced in this beautiful place with water rushing in the background, gentle oranges and yellows of a setting sun peeking through the trees, warm companionship with a fellow hiker, and a giggling game with the headset. It seemed this day had not been packed with normal hours, but with entire eras of time. Each era had been memorable, vibrant, so full of color and life and danger that I could scarcely believe we'd actually lived them.

I thought back to Week 1 and our first meeting with Gretchen, to that gorgeous sunset and the rows of mountains, all in different shades of purple. I thought of how I'd been scared to fall asleep with the Matrix-lovers talking violence in the tent next door. It seemed a different lifetime. I'd been someone younger back then.

We'd escaped with our lives today, and I was amazed at how quickly we'd moved on, like that terrifying moment had floated down the time stream and become just a story. We had ended the day in such a normal way. There was no dramatic aftermath, no gabbing to friends about how we'd "almost died!" There was no sitting down in my comfy chair at home and having a double Jack Daniel's and shaking my head at how close we'd come. There had just been more hiking, a brief mention of the incident to Mark, and that was it.

It was just... done now, just one of many things on the trail—a stern reminder to pay attention, for sure, but also a contrast that made the moments afterward that much richer. I felt as if my eyes had been opened wider to the beauty all around us.

I felt initiated, like we'd come through fire and it had changed us.

I pulled my cold feet into my sleeping bag at last, zipped up the side, and settled back with a smile. I felt, perhaps for the first time, like I actually belonged here.

And that night, I slept deeply.

16

WORLD WAR II BUNKER

THE MORNING DAWNED bright and cold. Once again, we weren't early risers. Waking Dash was a chore. Push. Prod. Yell. He would mumble and roll over many times before finally pulling himself from the tent. Still, he was amazingly good-natured about the whole thing. Rather than biting my head off for rousting him—as I would have done in his place—he actually tried to come up with helpful suggestions.

In the first week, after a few mornings of this long, drawn-out process, he'd told me, "Try shaking me."

I'd tried that. It hadn't worked.

"Maybe make the oatmeal first," he'd suggested. "Draw me out with the promise of food."

That hadn't worked.

Finally, yesterday morning as I'd harangued him to get out of bed—mere hours before the lightning on Searle Pass—he'd finally said, "Okay, you're going to have to get brutal, Dad. Strip the rain fly off while I'm still in there. Let out all the heat. If I'm so cold I get uncomfortable, that'll force me to get up."

So this morning, while he was mumbling and dozing, I

stripped off the wet rain fly, scattering icy droplets on him. And...

It didn't work.

In the end, I just prodded him over and over until he finally got his engine cranking.

It was endearing that he'd tried to solve the problem with me, like *he* wasn't the problem but that we were collaborating on how to rouse some *other* troublesome camper. I finally accepted that we were just going to be late risers. That's the way it was.

And it actually served as a reminder that this adventure wasn't about me. It was about Dash and his experience.

After I'd made breakfast, eaten, and packed my pack, I sat down to wait for him as he slowly got moving...

And I studied the hell out of the Data Book. There would be no repeats of yesterday. By the time we put our boots on the trail, I knew exactly where every water source was. I knew where every campsite was. And most importantly, I knew every piece of the trail that popped above eleven thousand seven hundred feet over the next seventy miles. As it turned out, there was only one, and we wouldn't reach it today. Today's hike was all forest and flat fields, far below tree line.

We came down out of the mountains onto a high plain with the sun shining brightly overhead, making good time. We passed the trailhead for Camp Hale and turned up Forest Service Road 714 for less than a mile, before heading off into a field toward a forest and an upward slope.

There was a little creek right before the woods, and we stopped, caught by an oddity off to our right. Of course, we had to investigate, and it turned out to be a concrete bunker as long as a football field with more than a dozen squat doorways.

What the hell was this doing way out here?

Someone had hauled up tons and tons of concrete to build this thing, and I was mystified as to its purpose. We wandered down the crumbling concrete path in front of the line of doorless doorways, stepping around bare Rebar sticking up here and there. We entered a few of the squat, square little cement rooms that looked tough enough to withstand a bomb. The walls were a foot thick.

The Data Book said they were "historic concrete bunkers," but I wasn't satisfied with that brief explanation. I checked my phone and, lo and behold, I had a signal. I immediately did some research.

This was a World War II compound, built in the 1940s to train American soldiers how to fight in the snow, to fight the Nazis in Scandinavia. Crazy.

As we explored those shoebox-sized cells, I imagined how training here must have been hell. Sleeping in freezing concrete boxes at night, snow training during the day.

My grandfather had been a tail gunner in World War II. He'd told me stories, and I never ceased to marvel at the things our soldiers went through. There were no safety catches or safety helmets back in those days. He flew time and again in a B-24 bomber, but they wouldn't even give him a parachute. I remember his story about when he'd first crawled into the tail gunner's seat and tried to pull a parachute in the cramped space with him.

"Can't go in there with a parachute," the instructor told him. "Won't fit."

"What happens if we get shot down and I have to jump out?" my grandfather asked.

The instructor just shrugged. "Don't get shot down."

That had been the kind of answer they could expect back then.

But grandfather wasn't satisfied with that answer, and he'd always been both a rebellious and resourceful sort. Instead of accepting his fate, he cut a two-foot length of rope, tied one end to his ankle and one to that parachute pack. He figured if he got blown out of the plane and was still alive, maybe the parachute would go with him. And maybe he'd have the time to pull it to him, put it on, and pull that ripcord before he hit the ground.

Maybe.

It wasn't good odds, but it was better odds, so he went

with it. The man didn't have any quit in him, and he'd never cozied up to authority figures. He didn't trust in "conventional wisdom" if he could think of a better alternative, and he loved to tinker with things, whether it was rules or cars or a tricycle made to look like a biplane for his grandkids. Maybe it was that irreverent, never-say-die attitude that accounted for his charmed life.

He survived World War II, flew thirty-one missions and lived to tell the tale. He married his high school sweetheart, sired my father shortly after the war, worked for the government until he retired at age fifty-five, and bought his dream house in El Toro, California. He watched his children and grandchildren grow up, celebrated his seventy-fifth wedding anniversary, and he died in his own bed a month shy of his one-hundred-and-fifth birthday.

We should all be that lucky.

I thought about my spectacular grandfather as I stared at that long line of squat concrete, about those World War II soldiers, about how different the world was back then. It was raw and unrefined, with edges not yet polished by generations of relative peace. There were no safety measures in place. Events were sharp enough to cut you to the bone. Courage and dumb luck were your best bets.

When I think of that, of my grandfather's world, part of me is glad I didn't have to face those same sharp edges. And yet, part of me is envious, too. I imagine the world as purer. Danger wasn't sugar-coated. Lies weren't ubiquitous. People's agendas were closer to the surface.

But maybe that's just my imagination running wild again.

As Dash and I walked away from those concrete bunkers, they lingered in my mind. I think about them still, about their testament to our past. I imagine they'll still be standing when my son is fifty, will still be whispering stories about World War II.

The trail continued over the river and up into the woods, and I was thankful for the incline. My feet, which I'd been so optimistic about when we'd started this second week, had taken a hit from our run yesterday, and they hurt more now than they had since the first week. About a mile later, after the uphill hike, we found a creek and I spent a few moments soaking my feet in icy water to keep the swelling down. A big freeze-out of the toes, then dry and bandage, and it was like I had new feet for the next half hour before the needles returned.

While Dash waited for me, he discovered the "panorama" feature on my iPhone. Turns out if you hold down the button and sweep the camera left to right, you can capture a three-hundred-and-sixty-degree view.

Dash, of course, explored every possibility and we soon discovered that, if I panned really slowly, Dash could start in the left-hand side of the shot, sprint behind me after the camera moved past him, and set up on the right-hand side just as my sweep reached its end. And *voila*! We had two Dash's in the picture.

Goofy antics quickly ensued. Silly faces. Contorted poses. Hiding in the trees as though a doppelganger had separated itself from him and dashed off to peek around a different trunk. We took many of these experimental shots.

Over the next few days, we fell into the rhythm of hiking and camping. Dash seemed as happy as I'd ever seen him. The discussion of "not finishing the trail" seemed like a distant memory.

After a week and a half, our experiences became a part of us. Yes, we'd made our mistakes, but we had also learned. And we had the Data Book down. We learned how to keep dry during the intermittent afternoon squalls while still forging ahead, when to put on rain gear and when to let the droplets fall on us and allow the sun to dry us out minutes later. I switched socks religiously, every hour or so. We planned our days, taking into account not only distance and water sources, but also elevation gain and loss, and we began to get a very accurate idea of what we could accomplish and how long it would take.

Unfortunately, my feet had stopped getting better. Maybe

the flight on Searle Pass had set them back, or maybe I just couldn't walk fifteen-plus miles every day and expect them to heal.

Still, it wasn't as bad as the first week because I had methods to deal with the pain now. Feet in creek. Moleskin and bandages. Keeping a constant rotation of dry socks. Popping ibuprofen. I managed to push the pain back just enough during the day to make it to camp. The nightly rests and chilling my feet against the drom gifted me two or maybe three good hours of hiking the next day before the pain set in.

If we'd only wanted to do about five to ten miles a day, I imagine my feet might have healed up on the trail. But Dash and I were pushing now. He wanted mileage and I was on board despite my injuries. If we were going to keep to our schedule—if we were going to get to Durango by the fifth week—we had to move faster.

We had averaged around eleven miles a day during the first week. In the second week, we did far better. We'd hiked thirteen miles the first day, sixteen miles the second day, and managed nineteen miles on the third day before darkness and rain forced us to stop.

The twenty-mile day remained a tantalizing goal, a unicorn we'd glimpsed but couldn't seem to catch.

But three days later, on Segment 11, we pushed hard and finally nabbed it.

On Segment 11, the trail drops down out of the mountains and runs alongside Highway 82 for about seven miles as it loops around the Twin Lakes. On that flat, we made our push for the goal.

Of course, there were other problems along that section of trail. Dash wrangled with ants. Apparently they loved the flat ground too. Perfect for making their copious anthills. He quickly discovered that when he stopped to wait for me, the ants wasted no time crawling up his boots and socks to get to the tender flesh of his calves.

As you might guess, that was the end of Dash waiting for me. He scooted ahead and continued to put distance between us until he reached a dam that crossed over the southeast side of the lake.

I set a pace that was doable for my feet and amused myself by watching families enjoy a summer day at the lake to my right. I began to dream of our next Zero Day, of cheeseburgers and fries. I thought a lot about food on the trail, but though I was eating far fewer calories than I was burning—and I was losing weight—I never felt malnourished. We had enough food now. It was just that it was all the same food, which made dreaming about things like cheeseburgers particularly satisfying.

We would camp tonight at the end of Segment 11, which left only the eighteen and a half miles of Segment 12 for tomorrow. That was a solid day, and there were two big mountains to climb, but it was well within our capabilities, especially with the paradise of a Zero Day on the other side.

I also dreamed of healing up. I'd come so close to making my feet right with just a single day in Breckenridge. Another Zero Day was going to make a world of difference for me. Two would be even better, but we could only afford the one. We were behind in our schedule. We'd already have to increase our pace over the next three weeks to reach Durango as planned. A fifteen-mile-a-day average was no longer enough to stay on target.

So one Zero Day was what it was. I just hoped it would be enough to kick this foot problem for good.

I finally caught up with Dash at the dam, where he'd found a chunk of concrete to stand upon to ward off the ants. As I reached him, the skies opened up, sending the summer lake-goers running for their RVs and tents. Dash and I just pulled out our rain gear and kept on hiking.

Once we got over the dam, it was lunch time, and we found a big tree with a dry patch beneath it, huddled under and had lunch in the rain.

Down the slope in a dirt parking lot, I saw a woman making food inside her RV, having lunch just like we were. She was warm and dry, tucked within her little bubble of civilization out here in the wild.

I thought I should feel envy at that, but I didn't. Instead, I felt a kind of invincibility. We were hunkering down in the rain, happily eating our lunch, like we were part of the forest. Like this was no big deal. We knew the storm would blow itself out soon, and we had the equipment to shrug it off.

I glanced at Dash, who chomped away, just being... Well, just *being*.

We hadn't run out into the wild for a week and come limping home. We were *actually doing this*. This had become...normal. We weren't just surviving. We were thriving. Each of us was a self-sustaining unit that could move at will through the wilderness.

Okay, I thought. *This is pretty damned cool.*

I felt a deep satisfaction, but it was more than that. We had achieved what we'd come for. This, right here, was the experience I'd hoped Dash would get.

We weren't visitors anymore. The trail had become a part of us.

17

THE ELECTRIC BLUE SHOES

WE FINISHED OUR LUNCH, got back on the trail, and cautiously climbed from the lake to a height of about ten thousand feet. The rain showers came and went, and though we never came close to tree line, I stayed alert as a hawk when we went up and over those ridges. I searched the skies, listened for thunder, checked for cover.

The leaden clouds hemmed and hawed. They showered us, then revealed the sun, then showered us again, then made way for the sun again.

After more than an hour with this schizophrenic squall, the rain started in earnest. By then we were only a few miles from our campsite, and we were sick of stopping every ten minutes to put on our rain pants, then stopping five minutes later to take them off again. We kept our rain jackets on, and of course we'd protected our packs, but we were done futzing with the rain pants. After all, the storm was going to quit again in a few minutes.

Except this time it didn't.

By the time we topped the final ridge of Segment 11 and

descended toward County Road 390, Dash and I were soaked from the waist down and shivering cold.

We crossed the highway, went about a tenth of a mile farther, and found the most beautiful campsite right next to Clear Creek. Giant, towering pines protected a perfect flat space next to the river. As an unexpected bonus, the cluster of pines towering over the campsite had protected a couple of thirty-foot circles of dry dirt from the deluge. We pitched our tent out of the rain and actually hung up our clothes along the trunks to let them dry out.

Once our wet clothes were hung and the tent was set up, we jumped inside. The only warmth to be had was our own body heat. We dried off as best we could, changed into dry clothing, tucked into our sleeping bags, and waited for our heat to fill the tent.

"This sucks," Dash said, teeth chattering.

"It'll warm up," I said.

"Yeah, and then we have eighteen and a half miles tomorrow. Two twelve-thousand-foot peaks. In the rain."

"The rain'll stop."

"It hasn't yet."

I began to wonder if he was right. The idea of hiking eighteen miles over two twelve-thousand-foot ridges tomorrow in the rain—not to mention possible lightning—was daunting.

"How close are we to Buena Vista?" Dash asked.

I checked the Data Book.

"Eighteen point five miles," I said. We were right by County Road 390, which undoubtedly led to Buena Vista. Dash took the Data Book from me, and I could see he was doing some figuring in his head.

"It's a twenty-minute drive to Buena Vista," he said, and I knew what he was thinking.

Lara's sister Carla and her husband Chris owned a condo in Buena Vista, and they had offered it as a stopping point for our second Zero Day. Lara had planned to come up a day earlier, spend some time alone, and then meet us at the Segment 13 trailhead tomorrow.

"She's probably there already," he said. He shivered, pulled his sleeping bag higher on his shoulders.

"We can't do that, buddy," I said.

"Why not?"

"Because we'd be skipping a part of the trail. Because it's Mom's alone time. Because we agreed to get out here and do this and we can't just cut the trail short."

"Except we can if we want to," he said.

I hated that he was right. My mind was set on hiking *every* part of the trail. I didn't want to just skip a segment because it got a little rainy and a little cold.

But the truth was, we could swap Segment 12 for an extra Zero Day in Buena Vista and still stay on schedule. And my feet could really use that extra day. I imagined what it might be like if they had two full days. That might be all I needed to have normal feet for the next three weeks.

I listened to the rain outside, which gave no signs of stopping. It was already six-thirty. The reason the afternoon thunderstorm caution was from noon to four was because most storms stopped by then.

What if it *did* just continue raining? What would that do to my feet to hike that far sloshing around in my boots? My switching-socks system required hot sunlight to dry out the spares on the back of my pack. Without the sun, there'd be no switching socks.

But I shook that away. I'd gone six days. I could go one more, no matter the conditions. We'd already skipped Segment 1. We couldn't possibly skip another. That wasn't thru-hiking.

Dammit, we'd committed to this. We'd just have to stick it out—

"Dad," Dash interrupted softly, as though he could read my mind. "This trip is supposed to be about having fun. Are you going to have fun if you have to hike through this tomorrow? Are you honestly?"

"It's not just about fun. It's about doing what we said we were going to do. If we don't hike all the segments, we're not really hiking the trail."

But even as I said it, it sounded silly. Not really hiking the trail... We'd already put in almost two hundred miles. Two hundred miles! How was that NOT hiking the trail?

Was my reluctance about wanting to be able to tell my friends that we'd hiked the entire thing? What the hell was that? Bragging rights?

"It *is* about having fun," Dash said. "I don't care about skipping a segment. Does it really matter that much?"

I stayed silent for a long time. Finally, I mumbled, "I don't even know if we can get a signal out here."

He raised an eyebrow at the crack in my resolve, and he glanced at the pocket where I kept my phone.

I pulled it out. It had died midday, but I had one quarter of a charge on the portable recharge battery I carried. I'd been saving it for the end of Segment 12.

"We'll have to use up the charge," I said. "If there's no signal, we're screwed." We wouldn't be able to call Lara tomorrow night at the planned rendezvous point.

But I began to get behind the new plan. The idea of sleeping in a warm bed, hanging up the Cruel Shoes and resting my feet...

"Okay. Let's give it a try," I said.

"Yes!" He gave a fist pump in his sleeping bag, making him look like a giant wiggling worm.

I charged the phone. When the remote battery died, my phone had a fourteen percent charge...

And I had two bars. I made the call.

Lara picked up on the third ring. She didn't ask us about skipping the segment. She didn't encourage us to stick it out. She didn't complain that we'd spoiled her alone time. Her boy and her man were stuck in a storm, cold and wet and asking for help.

She simply said, "Where are you?"

I told her.

"Be there in twenty minutes." She hung up.

Remember how I'd mentioned that it took Dash and me a good hour to break down camp each morning? Yeah. We had that camp down in fifteen minutes. Dash literally ran the tenth of a mile to the road. I limped after.

I crested the small rise and there it was: our boxy taupe Toyota Sienna mini-van. At that moment, I'd never seen a more beautiful car. Lara had the hatchback open for me by the time I reached her. I unclipped my pack, tossed it in the back and kissed her.

"You're amazing," I murmured.

"You're soaked," she said, smiling. "You okay?"

"Glad for the rest. Grateful for the rescue. You're my hero, Ferris Bueller."

She winked and drove us to Buena Vista.

That night, once we'd had our showers—oh, that glorious shower—we feasted on cheeseburgers and Cokes. I thought that maybe I'd pick up a taste for something else on the first meal of my second Zero Day. I was wrong. Cheeseburgers and Coke. That's all I wanted.

Scrubbed and bandaged, I put my feet up and we all watched Monty Python's *The Holy Grail*. It rained the rest of that night.

As King Arthur methodically chopped the arms off the Black Knight, I thought about our decision to skip Segment 12. We may not have completed another segment, but I *had* listened to Dash. Rather than indulging my competitive drive, I'd fulfilled a promise of a different kind. My promise to my son, to make this about us. I'd come out here to be with him. To listen to him. To bond.

During and after the movie, Dash remained plugged into his phone, catching up with his friends through a flurry of online exchanges as he'd done in Breckenridge.

For two days, we luxuriated. My feet had a chance to heal. I ate more M&Ms and drank more Cokes than a person ought to. And most importantly, I ditched the Cruel Shoes at last. I figured two weeks and two hundred miles was plenty of time to break in a pair of shoes. The verdict? The Cruel Shoes refused to be broken in, and I wasn't going to walk another step in them. I went down to the local Buena Vista sporting goods store, The Trailhead, to see what my alternatives were, and I talked for a while with the shoe sales attendant.

"I'm not sure hiking boots are working for me," I told him. "So I have a question for you."

"Okay," he said.

"Why would I choose hiking boots over a pair of tennis shoes?" I asked.

"Well, ankle support. It's critical."

I'd heard this before. Ankle support. Ankle support. Ankle support. This was not a new refrain. I said, "You know, I'm not sure I believe that."

"Well, your ankles need support..." he said, not sure where I was going with this. He said it like it was common knowledge, like he was saying, "Gravity makes things fall to the floor. Everybody knows that."

And maybe it *was* common knowledge. But as I mentioned before, I'm not a big fan of trusting "common knowledge" in the first place, just because everybody seems to know it. Every person is different, and I'd spent a few weeks experiencing all kinds of troubles with hiking boots. I had real foot troubles, and I had no desire to swap out my current problem for a similar problem. And I had never, ever, on this hike or during any of my previous hikes, said to myself, "Oh, my aching ankles. I sure wish they had more support."

Not once.

Still, I remained polite. "I'm not sure ankle support is important to me," I said pleasantly. "I'm more concerned with a cushy sole. What else do you have?"

"Well...hiking boots are really what you want for hiking."

"What about trail runners?" I asked.

"Well, they're good for running trails, but I don't know that I'd recommend them for long-distance hiking with a heavy pack. They have no ankle support."

If he said ankle support one more time... I flicked my annoyance to the back of my mind.

"Let's pretend ankle support doesn't matter in this case," I said. "Can I try some trail runners instead?" I asked.

"Sure," he said.

I pointed at a gray pair of trail runners—which looked like glorified running shoes. "Can I try those?" I looked and saw a red pair with black soles. "And maybe those. And…" I searched. There was an electric blue pair, too. They seemed pretty ostentatious for my taste. But what the hell. "And that one." I pointed.

Without any further argument, he went downstairs to get them in my size, and I sat waiting.

The attendant came back with three boxes. I put on the first pair.

Nope.

Ouch and ouch. I took them off. The upside of my blisters, I supposed, was that I knew in an instant that the shoe wasn't going to work.

I thought about my experiment back in Breckenridge… What if *every* pair of shoes felt horrible? I mean, I'd tried on all of the shoes I'd owned. And those were shoes that had already been broken in with my own feet.

I picked up the next pair, the red with the black soles, and I put them on.

Nope.

I took them off.

I let out a breath, beginning to despair. Maybe I needed to come to the realization that I'd destroyed my feet, and nothing was going to set it right. Maybe I was going to have to soldier on with the Cruel Shoes after all.

I picked up the last pair, the electric blue Altra Olympus 4 trail runners, and I put them on.

No pain.

I moved my feet around a little. Nothing but cushy, marshmallow relief.

"Oh my…" I drew in a little breath, standing up. My feet sank down like they were on orthopedic beds made just for them. The shoes. Didn't. Hit. My blisters. At all.

At all!

"Oh this is a miracle," I murmured, walking back and

forth. It was like the shoe had been designed to avoid all of the tender spots on my foot. "It can't be real." I walked around the store, waiting for the pain to return. It didn't. It seemed…impossible.

"I'll take them," I said, boxed up my old shoes, went to the counter and slapped down my credit card.

"They're a hundred and sixty-four dollars," he said.

"I don't care if they're a thousand and sixty-four dollars," I replied. Oh, the freedom! I imagined hiking the trail and not having to worry about my feet. That was a dream, some misty fantasy I'd stopped believing in a long time ago, but now it was possible! I kept thanking the attendant and grinning and thanking the attendant and signing the credit card slip and thanking the attendant. The shoes were heaven.

I wore those suckers home. I wore them everywhere. They were even better than walking on bare feet!

I practically skipped back to the condo.

Though most of my attention was dedicated to power lounging during our two Zero Days, and letting my feet rest even more, I did have *some* work to do. I posted our previous weeks' journey on Facebook, and then I considered the trail ahead.

When we'd begun, I really didn't know if we'd get this far, but now that we were a mere thirty-three-point-three miles from the midway point, it was time to etch our plan in stone. If Dash and I continued on, we'd have to make arrangements with other people to help us with our fourth and fifth food drops.

Lara had agreed to support us through next week, Zero Day #3. The pull-out point was an hour's drive from Buena Vista at the end of Segment 17. She'd said she'd make that drive, take us back to Buena Vista for our third Zero Day, then put us back on the trail. But after that, we'd have to find another way to make the final two food drops, and if we wanted another Zero Day, we'd have to work out the lodging ourselves.

Here's where I mention that I'm surrounded by amazing

friends and family, in case that wasn't already apparent. When I'd mentioned hiking The Colorado Trail, my stepsister Nancy and her husband Robert—who live in Durango—had immediately offered to house us at the end of the trail. Nancy had also offered to drive up to Molas Pass and deliver the final food drop that would feed us on our last week of the trail.

That left Lake City, the second-to-last food drop, which was halfway between the Segment 18 trailhead and Molas Lake. All I had to do was find someone willing to drop food there or, failing that, ask Lara to mail it to the Lake City post office where we could pick it up.

I called Nancy, gabbed with her for half an hour—it's never hard to talk to Nancy—and she reaffirmed her commitment for both Molas Pass and Durango. Not only that, but her daughter, Raeden, reaffirmed that she wanted to join our little group at Molas Pass and hike the last leg of the trail with us.

I hung up with her, and that's when an angel dropped out of the sky.

A.J. Johnson, a friend of mine from way back in second grade at Riverview Elementary School in Durango, had seen my most recent Facebook post. In a comment, he'd expressed wild enthusiasm for our undertaking. An avid hiker, A.J. lived in Texas, and he went into the wilderness every chance he got.

Also in his comment, he asked if he could do anything to help us. Food drop. Picking us up at a trailhead. He even expressed interest in hiking part of the CT with us.

I called him up, and he said he was actually going to be traveling from Texas to Durango for family matters during the time we'd be heading past Lake City. He offered to drive up there, bring our food, take us into town for a quick overnight stay, and then hike with us for a portion of the next day.

We firmed up the details of the plan, I hung up with A.J. and sat back. Wow.

And that was that. We were going all the way. I think until that moment, I'd harbored the possibility that we might not make it, that the plan might fall apart somehow. But now that

I'd committed other people to this endeavor, I wasn't about to let them down. They were going to do their part. I damn well better do mine.

Unbeknownst to me, the entire remainder of our trip was balanced on the edge of a knife.

And there was nothing I could do to alter the outcome.

18
DASH'S DECISION

WHILE I WAS BUSY confirming food drops and warm receptions, Dash was getting reacquainted with his friends back home and fostering his longing for a normal summer.

After the first day, I didn't really notice when his mood began to darken. I was reveling in M&Ms, Cokes, and burgers. I was healing, preparing, soaking up the blessed laziness of our Zero Days. And he didn't say anything to indicate he was upset.

In retrospect, his silence should have tipped me off.

On the afternoon of our second and final Zero Day in Buena Vista, I was organizing our food stuffs into piles. One would stay here for our third rest when Lara brought us back from the end of Segment 17, one would be mailed out to A.J. for Lake City, and the final food drop would be mailed to Nancy in Durango for her trip to Molas Lake.

I'd just put on the finishing touches, adding extra beef jerky—we'd never once had enough beef jerky on the trail.

Dash came out of his room, a frown on his face. And this time, I did notice.

"What's up, buddy?" I asked.

"Well, you're just... I mean, you're getting everything prepared," he said.

That statement made my heart sink. There was only one reason he'd be upset about me prepping, and that was if he'd decided he wasn't going.

"Ah," I said.

"I'm not sure I want to keep going," he said.

Bingo.

"I see."

He didn't need to give me the reasons why. He'd done that in Breckenridge.

I thought back to that moment now, about how he felt he was missing his entire summer with his friends. I also, of course, recalled my promise. I'd said I wouldn't guilt him, wouldn't shame him, wouldn't manipulate him in any way. I'd told him it would be his decision.

But I was disappointed. After the amazing times we'd had this past week, after everything we'd been through and how much he'd loved the trail, I was almost sure we'd moved past this. It was like he was two people—Trail Dash and City Dash. When he was out there, he loved it. But when he got back to the city, he changed.

I took a deep breath.

My next impulse was to say something like, "Dash, I watch you on the trail, and you're so happy." Or, "We're past the hard part. We're thirty-three-point-three miles from the halfway point, and you're hiking eighteen to twenty miles a day. You're finally acclimated. You want to give up *now*?"

I didn't say any of that. That was a guilt trip. I'd be cajoling him to see my side. And I'd promised I wouldn't.

I suddenly realized that this was the moment, that this entire enterprise was going to come down to this one decision. We'd either continue the trail or stop now, based on how this moment played out. And I couldn't do anything to nudge it my way.

After a moment, I said, "Okay. Tell you what. You take

thirty minutes to think about it. Mom and I will meet you in the living room in exactly thirty minutes, and you can give us your final decision."

He looked at me with narrowed eyes. "Really?"

I nodded. "Really."

"And that's it?"

"And that's it."

He continued looking at me like he didn't quite believe me but couldn't see where the trick was. Then he walked into his room and shut the door.

I stopped organizing the food and retreated to the master bedroom. Lara, who had overheard everything from the kitchen, followed me and closed the door softly behind herself.

One look at her face and I knew Dash wasn't my only problem now. While I wasn't going to spend time convincing him to continue with the trail, I was going to have to convince Lara that we couldn't push him. She hadn't been there during my conversation with Dash as we climbed out of Breckenridge. She hadn't made my same promise.

And she had invested in this enterprise too. She'd driven to Breckenridge, brought us food, took care of us. And let's not forget about the financial commitment. With all the equipment, food, lodging and travel expenses, we were in for close to three thousand dollars.

She's going to tell me I can't let him quit, I thought.

"You can't just let him quit," she said.

"I have to," I said. "If that's what he wants."

"You *have* to?"

"I promised him."

Staring into her expectant face, all of my doubts returned. I thought about forcing Dash to the top of Mt. Bierstadt. He would never have done that if I hadn't stayed the course. Shouldn't I approach this the same way? Maybe he wasn't old enough yet for me to assume this had to be his decision.

I thought of how we'd skipped Segment 12, how that had probably set up a precedent. My fault. I mean, if we could skip two segments, why not skip the rest? We had hiked from

Denver to Buena Vista. That was pretty impressive all by itself.

Just like climbing thirteen thousand five hundred feet of a 14'er was impressive.

"He has come two weeks and nearly two hundred miles to get here," Lara said. "You're just going to let him say, 'Forget it. I wanna go home?'"

"Yes." I let out a breath. "I have to. I told him that this would be his decision. I have to let him make it."

Her brow was furrowed, and she'd pressed her lips into a defiant line. She was not one for shouting matches. She wasn't going to argue, but it was clear she didn't agree with me.

Despite my worries, despite her disapproval, I felt a rightness in my belly. Perhaps Dash was a bit young to make this decision, but we don't always get to choose when we reach a threshold. I certainly hadn't when I was fourteen.

"I have to let him," I said to her earnestly. "For his sake. Do you see?"

"For his sake?"

"He's a smart kid. I mean, a really smart kid. He predicted all of this as we were hiking up out of Breck. He knew I'd want to force him to continue."

"So he got you to promise him," she said. I wasn't the only one who knew our child.

"Yes. He did."

"So maybe he's manipulating you."

"Doesn't matter," I said.

"I don't see how that doesn't matter."

"It doesn't matter because he's right."

She didn't say anything, but I could see her stubbornness ease up.

"He is having an amazing time, Lara," I said softly. "He's truly happy in the woods. It's like he's made for it. His body eats up the exercise and asks for more. He breathes in that fresh air, those beautiful vistas, and it feeds him. He's his ideal self out there." I paused. "And he knows it."

"It doesn't sound like he knows it."

"He's facing a challenge. The CT, wonderful as it is, is a

ton of work. Every day. Sun up to sun down. Going home means cheeseburgers and video games and lazy days with friends. Come on, even you would have a tough time with that choice."

She let out a breath and looked pensive.

"He has to see it for himself," I continued. "If I make him go, he'll fight me every step of the way. If he decides to go, it's all on him. And when he finishes the trail, it's going to be *his* triumph. He'll never wonder, 'Would I really have finished if my Dad hadn't pushed me?'"

She glanced at the door, thinking.

"This is the most important lesson of the entire trail," I said. "This. Right now."

"What if he says he won't continue?" she asked.

I swallowed. That was my worst fear. Because it was more likely than not that he *would* say that. "Then…we have to let him. And I guess it becomes a different kind of lesson."

"I don't like that lesson," she said.

"I don't like it either, but I honestly don't think we get a choice. That's the point."

I felt like she understood what I was doing here, and she finally nodded.

After half an hour, she and I went out and sat on the couch. Dash came out a few minutes later, and I could see the war on his face. He looked angry, and he flopped down on the couch opposite us.

I wanted to say half-a-dozen things. I held them all back and waited. Lara, as always, knew the value of when not to talk, and she stayed silent too.

"I don't like this," Dash said.

"Having to decide?" I asked.

"Well, I mean, if I say I don't want to go, you're going to be upset. And you've already called Nancy and that friend of yours and set up the food. So what are they going to think of me?"

"Nope," I said. "Don't put this on them. Plans are made, but plans can be changed. I can make calls and cancel things.

Nothing is set in stone."

"But you're going to be upset," he said.

"Yeah. I will be. I may even decide to continue the trail on my own. But don't put this on me, either. I told you this would be your decision, and it is. You stop the trail now, you get to go home and play video games and hang out with your friends. You'll get the normal summer you've been wanting. But you won't get to see the rest of the trail. You won't get to say you finished it. And okay, yeah, you may disappoint Nancy and A.J. But if you continue on the trail, you'll disappoint your friends at home. Any decision you make is going to have its pleasure and its price."

The next moment seemed to last a long time. It was excruciating to just sit back and wait for the axe to fall. I honestly didn't know what he would do. And there were a hundred little things I could say to bump him over the line, subtle things. It would barely be cheating. Just a little nudge to make him choose to keep going.

I stayed silent.

During this seemingly interminable effort to keep my lips locked, I began to feel a certain pride. There would be no cajoling. No spin on the facts. No matter what happened, I could honestly say I'd let him make his own choice.

"Well, I guess I'll keep going," he finally said, not sounding the least bit enthusiastic.

I held his gaze and he held mine. I waited for the count of two heartbeats, then I nodded. "Okay."

Lara and I went back into the bedroom, and we both did a ridiculous and silent happy dance. He'd decided to keep going, and I knew that if we made it through Week 3, we weren't going to face this crossroads again.

As I'd predicted, his decision was the turning point. But what was coming next would change us both forever, and it would become my favorite moment on the trail.

19

MY FAVORITE MOMENT

I DON'T THINK even Dash knew which way he would come down before he made his decision. He'd struggled with it beforehand, and he struggled with it afterward. That war showed on his face as we loaded our packs and Lara drove us to the trailhead. He was sullen, and he didn't want to talk.

I maintained my original stance: I needed to get him to the trail, just needed a few miles between us and the city.

As fate would have it, the dirt road that led up to the trailhead had been washed out from the last two days of heavy rains. It was already a relatively bumpy road with occasional deep ruts—nothing that Lara, an experienced country and snow driver, couldn't handle.

But when we came around that last bend, one of the ruts had been carved out by what must have been a small river the day before. If we'd had a four-wheel-drive, we could have gotten over it, but the clearance on the mini-van simply wasn't going to make it.

"It's just a couple miles to the trailhead," I said. "We can walk. It'll warm us up."

Dash's frown smashed down a little more. He kicked open the door, jumped out of the car, snatched his pack and started stomping up the trail.

I gave Lara a kiss.

"He doesn't look happy," she said.

"Nope."

She seemed like she wanted to say more, but didn't.

"I love you," I said. "Thank you for everything. Drive safe."

"I will."

She drove away.

Unlike the previous three times Lara drove away, I didn't feel even a momentary longing at her departure, nor a scrap of doubt. This was where I wanted to be, and my body was doing better all the time. Besides, an event was mounting, and I wanted my full attention on it. Dash was like a pressure cooker, ready to pop his lid. I needed to be prepared. No time for looking backward. Only forward.

I started up the dirt road after him.

We'd planned sixteen and a half miles today, a nice beginning to our third week. All of a sudden, that sixteen-and-a-half mile day had turned into an eighteen-and-a-half mile day. I'm not gonna lie, that extra two miles was rough. Walking through the wilderness energizes the soul, but walking down a dirt road through a mountain suburb for no extra gain just plain sucks.

In other words, between his "Well, I guess I'll keep going" decision and this less-than-glamorous beginning, Dash was miserable.

I was in high spirits. For the first time since we'd started this journey, I felt like I knew what I was doing and that I was up to the task. My feet felt fabulous; no pain management. That left some emotional bandwidth to respond properly to Dash's dark mood, rather than snapping at him to suck it up. Even the boring stretch of dirt road didn't get me down.

The farther we went up that dirt road, the angrier Dash got. He began to rail against everything.

"Argh! These shoes are too loose! What the hell?" He stopped, re-tied them, walked for a while.

"Dammit! Now they're too tight!" He stopped again and messed with them some more. I waited patiently.

Once he fixed his shoes, he stomped on ahead. Now he began tugging on the straps of his pack.

"I had this adjusted just right before Buena Vista! Now these straps aren't right." He yanked on them, stopped, took off his pack, re-adjusted, then threw it back onto his back. Shortly after, he practically shouted as he wrestled with the straps again.

"This is the stupidest thing ever!" he said. "I hate this." I wasn't sure if he meant the pack or the trail.

I waited.

"This was a mistake," he said finally, perhaps thinking he was clueing me in to the fact that he was upset. "I don't want to be here."

With every comment he made, I saw an opportunity to interpose myself, to try to explain to him that he was just readjusting after having two days off, to point out that he was bummed because we weren't to the trailhead yet. I could have tried to remind him of the previous week, convince him that everything would be better once we were in the woods.

And I had the sense that he *wanted* me to. He wanted me to say something so he could push back against it, contradict it. If he could fight me, it would be easier than fighting himself.

I didn't give him the opportunity. I kept my mouth shut and let him have his space. I even fell back a bit, letting a dozen paces separate us as he cursed and spat and struggled. A part of me wondered if I was wrong. What if this was the new Dash for the rest of the trail? What if he was going to curse and spit and struggle for the next hundred miles? Ugh.

But about a half mile from the trailhead, he got quiet. He stopped struggling with his pack, stomping his feet, or growling at me. He just walked in silence like I was doing. I assumed he'd taken the fight inside his head.

Finally, we reached the trailhead, a well-groomed dirt

parking lot with a sparkling new restroom structure. This excited me. My least favorite part of camping was digging my own latrines every morning. Any chance to use a real restroom was an opportunity not to be missed.

Dash had been quiet long enough. It was time to test the waters. Maybe I could talk to him without an immediate explosion.

"Hey look," I said. "It's the last restroom for a while. Wanna go first?"

He stopped hiking, looking straight forward but not at me. I waited for a sarcastic jab.

He shook his head, and then he did look up at me. "No," he said softly. "I need to go sit by the river and get myself together."

That surprised me. "Oh?"

"Yeah."

"Okay, buddy."

He headed off toward the little bridge that spanned North Cottonwood Creek. After doing my business and exiting the restroom, I glanced around but couldn't find him. I wasn't in a hurry. It seemed like he wanted to calm down, and as far as I was concerned, we could stay by the river for an hour if he wanted.

Another hiker was sitting on a rock with her feet in the river, so I stopped and chatted with her about the balm of cold river water on tired feet. She was a young woman with a thick blonde braid slung over one shoulder, a short runner's cap pulled low on her forehead, and a black brace on her left knee. Her trail name was, appropriately, River Dip, and we talked for a brief moment before Dash re-appeared.

"That your son?" she asked.

"He's mine, yep."

"You thru-hiking?"

"All the way to Durango," I said. For the first time, I really believed it.

"That's a pretty cool thing to do," she said.

"Aw, thanks."

She seemed nice, but I got the impression that I was interrupting her meditative moment, so I wished her happy hiking and went to Dash, who was waiting a short distance up the trail. He seemed pensive.

"You okay?" I asked as we started walking.

He looked back the way we'd come like he was looking back in time. "Yeah, I…I just needed to spend a little time alone."

"Sure," I said.

He shook his head like he couldn't figure something out, and then he said, "I was being a baby back there."

My eyebrows raised.

"Somehow, in Buena Vista, I lost my meditative mindset. When I'm on the trail, I'm calm. But in the city…. It's crazy. I don't know what it is. Maybe it's being around my electronics or something, but it turns me into a different person." He shook his head. "And that guy back there who was yelling and complaining and stuff…that *me* back there, I don't like that guy. I don't want to be that guy, and I don't know why I was. I want to be the guy I am on the trail. I can think here. I can organize my thoughts."

I stumbled, absolutely gobsmacked. I mean, I'd hoped that Dash would pull himself together eventually, maybe after half a day or so, but in my wildest dreams I hadn't imagined he would do it like this. So quickly. So completely. He'd just consciously plucked himself out of his bad mood, identified the problem, and fixed it.

It was such an adult move, I was rendered speechless. Hell, it was more than just an adult move. Most adults didn't have that kind of personal insight or self-honesty, let alone the ability to pull off that transformation.

"Well…." I finally managed to speak. "That's just…amazing."

He didn't like listening to big speeches or lectures—and he didn't like to give them. He also didn't like bragging, either on himself, or when Lara and I bragged *about* him.

So he didn't respond to my compliment. He just turned

and started hiking up the trail. He'd said his piece. He was moving on. No need to make a big deal out of it.

I'd have to be astonished all by myself, in the quiet of my own mind. I mean, I'd just watched my kid grow up. Like, in one instant. Boom.

Anyone who knows me knows I'm a big fan of Blake Snyder's *Save the Cat*, an instructional book about the art of screenwriting. If you watch movies—even if you're not a writer—I recommend this book. It's like peeking past the curtain at all the levers and gears behind every movie you've ever loved.

If you're a writer and you haven't read it, well, good lord. Get thee to a bookstore. Don't make the same mistake I did and wait decades before opening that little treasure.

Anyway, as Dash hiked to his now-normal place twenty paces ahead of me, I immediately thought of Blake Snyder's comments on coming-of-age movies, how in a movie they show the coming-of-age process happening over a short span like, say, part of a school year—*The Karate Kid*—or even over a single Saturday in detention—*The Breakfast Club*. But in reality, a real-life person's coming of age happens over about five years. They just speed things up in a movie because they have to work the transformation in less than two hours.

But I suddenly felt like I was *in* a movie, that I'd watched some Hollywood rendition of a coming-of-age transformation. Except this wasn't Hollywood. This was *real*.

Just like the moment when I'd decided to become a magic hunter.

I thought back to my own fourteen-year-old transformation, standing on that precipice over the Animas River, deciding on the kind of man I wanted to be.

One of the daydreams I'd had when deciding to hike The Colorado Trail was getting to be there for my son at that same fourteen-year-old moment. He wouldn't be lost and alone with no safety net. He'd have me standing by his side.

But I'd long since learned that daydreams are only daydreams. Life doesn't follow a script. Except, of course, on those rare moments when it *does*. Damn!

I spent the next hour quietly jubilant.

Our journey had already been packed with glorious adventures, but this was the moment I'd really come for.

Still, it wouldn't be the most dramatic one. That was ahead of us, and Dash was about to show me how he could take charge when I faltered.

20
BALDY LAKE

IN THE SPIRIT of pure enjoyment, we decided to let go of our eighteen-and-a-half mile goal for the day. Instead, we hiked a sedate nine miles and cherry-picked our campsite. We chose a sweet spot in the warmth of early afternoon, leisurely filtered water from a stream about a tenth of a mile away, and just basked in the sun with no time pressure. We were delighted about an hour later when River Dip showed up and asked if she could join our campsite for the night.

After she'd assembled her tent, a compact little set-up that used her hiking poles as tent poles, we gathered together and shared dinner. I'd also seen her fill her bear bag earlier and hang it on a low branch. It rested against the trunk within easy reach of person or bear. After my day-by-day elaborate bear bag hanging system, seeing such sloppy bear bag treatment piqued my curiosity. I didn't get it.

"What's...uh... What's that?" I asked, pointing at her bear bag.

She gave me a glance like she wasn't sure what I was talking about. "My Ursack?" she asked.

Ah! So it was a thing. It wasn't a sloppy bear bag hang. It was intentional.

"What's an Ursack?" I asked.

"You've never seen an Ursack before?"

"My first one." I smiled. She smiled back and explained to me.

Turns out, the Ursack is a new take on the bear issue. Instead of suspending any old bag out of a bear's reach, Ursack lets the bear have the bag—but makes the bag indestructible. It's like a bear canister, except light and foldable so a hiker can reasonably add it to their kit.

An Ursack is made from Ultra High Molecular Weight Polyethylene, or UHMWPE, a lightweight modern marvel with a strength-to-weight ratio eight times that of high-strength steel. It's what they use to make U.S. Military body armor and protective jackets for fencers.

The upside was pretty obvious. Hanging a bear bag becomes a five-minute process, rather than a thirty-minute athletic feat. But there is a downside. If a bear does get hold of the bag, he's going to squash every bit of food you have trying to rip it open.

At dinner, we shared our Harmony House entree, and River Dip shared precious pieces of chocolate. Dash fell back into his trail personality. He was engaging and open, and he only fumbled for words once: after talking extensively about his frustrations with teachers, he found out River Dip was a middle school orchestra teacher. The awkward moment quickly devolved into laughter, but it was amazing to see how, up until that moment, age and rank hadn't mattered at all on the trail. We were all thru-hikers, bound by a common thread.

The next day, we hiked with River Dip for a while. We took pictures and exchanged information, promising we'd stay in touch before our differing hiking paces pulled us apart.

To River Dip: See? I did write the book. I promise the next one will have a female protagonist. ;)

The days that passed as we hiked Week 3 were some of the best of the trail. Our legs had acclimated. My feet were happy most of the time, and I actually began to challenge Dash when it came to hiking on the flats as well as the inclines, though declines were still tough for me, despite my magic blue shoes.

Throughout the week, we had more fantastic interactions. We met such colorfully-named hikers as Pufferbelly and Northstar. Tailwind and Starfail. GG and Triple Z. One of them, Timewarp, was thru-hiking the trail in Tevas. When I—now intensely interested in hiker footwear—asked him about his choice, he simply said, "My feet sweat. Can't wear shoes. This is the only thing I can wear that keeps them dry."

"And it's enough support for your ankles?" I asked.

"Never had a problem with ankle support." He shrugged. "But I've played the blister game, and I hate it."

I pointed at him. "Me too!"

He smiled and went on his way, and I fell to thinking about that. Everybody's different. Ankle problems for some. Blister problems for others. For my part, I decided I was bringing Tevas on my next big hike to test Timewarp's theory. If he could do it, I could do it too.

Dash and I met Tailwind and Starfail as we hiked through a field of wildflowers bursting with purples, pinks, oranges, blues. I'd never seen so many wildflowers in one place before. The colors just went on and on. I felt like I was standing in the middle of a Van Gogh painting.

Tailwind and Starfail were nice college-aged women. They only paused for a moment to chat with us, as they had miles to make that day. They were Northbounders, starting in Durango and ending in Denver. After they left, Dash and I soaked in the beauty of the wildflower field.

"We have to bring Mom back here," Dash said. "She's got to see this."

We added it to the list.

Speaking of lists, as we tromped along, we orchestrated a new list: the delicacies of an imaginary feast when we reached Durango. The feast—which we imagined eating all at once—looked like this:

- Swiss cheese turkey burger with bacon and mushrooms on top (of course)
- Giant fountain Coke (of course, again)
- Orange cream soda
- Caesar salad
- Fries, lots of fries (of course, once more)
- Fruit salad
- Some kind of spinach walnut Gorgonzola strawberry salad
- Mangoes!
- Sushi – California rolls, Philadelphia rolls, doesn't matter which rolls
- Chicken Alfredo mac & cheese
- Lemon pie with hardened chocolate on the top
- Key-lime pie
- Special homemade ice cream
- Creamy cherry ice cream
- Bacon-wrapped shrimp
- Salt water taffy
- Apple fritter
- Cheese Danish

Dash became inventive, imagining his ultimate hiker's chicken sandwich. A fried chicken patty covered with Alfredo mac 'n cheese and bacon. I laughed and said if he made it, I'd eat it.

As the hours and days and nights rolled on, Dash and I found we were excellent company for one another. Oh sure, from time to time we'd have arguments or get prickly, but mostly we joked, came up with verbal games, pointed out interesting VAMs (View Appreciation Moments), and most of all, enjoyed the quiet camaraderie of hiking through nature.

We passed the two-hundred-mile mark and celebrated by clicking selfies, each holding up two fingers like a peace sign.

When we passed the halfway mark of the entire trail shortly after, I felt a weight lift from my shoulders. We weren't "ramping up" anymore. When you make it halfway, you know you have what it takes to go all the way. There was nothing to prove anymore, no *I wonder if we're going to be able to make it.*

The final night of Week 3 put us at Baldy Lake. As a deep woods camping experience, it had everything. First of all, getting to the lake was an adventure in itself. It was off-trail about half a mile, so it probably wouldn't have been as popular if it wasn't so damned beautiful…and the only water source for twenty-four miles. The path dropped a precipitous four hundred feet in elevation down a steep winding stair-step that opened onto the majestic mountain lake.

Fed by melting snow from the ridges all around, Baldy Lake was so clear it looked like glass. Even twenty feet out, I could see straight to the bottom. I didn't see any obvious single stream leading into the lake—moving streams being my preferred source of water—so Baldy Lake became the first still body of water I used as a drinking source, run through the Platypus first, of course.

There were a number of fantastic campsites close by, and being the first hikers there that afternoon, we had our pick. In the end, rather than choosing to be right next to the water, we picked our spot slightly up the slope. It was perfect, and obviously loved by previous campers as it came complete with little rain trenches dug around the space for the tent. The view was breathtaking. We could see the lake, the trees clustered around it, and the ridges that rose in a bowl shape behind it.

That night, as Dash scampered down the tumbledown boulder slope to explore the area, he invited two campers we had met earlier that day on the trail to join us for dinner. Before today, Jack and Jamil had been strangers, both to each other and to us, but that night we talked and laughed like old friends until the sun went down, supping on hot meals over the JetBoil.

Jack had recently been laid off during the COVID slump, and he'd decided to make the most of his down time by hiking the CT. Jamil was an experienced hiker from New York who chose a different trail every summer, and this year's choice was the CT. He'd already hiked the Appalachian Trail and many others.

Dash and I talked about our adventures, about Searle Pass, the glory of Zero Days, and our increasing struggle to eat enough. I'd bolstered our food supplies before we started Week 3, but even with that, we were still famished all the time.

"That's hiker hunger," Jamil said. Apparently there was a name for this constant, low-grade hunger. He said it struck all long-range hikers eventually, usually in the third week, and at that point one simply could not stuff enough food in one's mouth to feel full.

Once the sun went down, the gentle temperature plummeted. We all stuck it out for a while, blowing warmth on our fingers and sipping hot chocolate, because we enjoyed the company, but we finally decided to call it a night.

As Jack stood up, he turned to Dash, "Hey, I've got an extra power bar or two, if you want them."

At the mention of extra food, Dash immediately perked up. Then, after a moment's hesitation, he shook his head. "No, no. I don't want to take your food."

"No, really," Jack said. "I packed too much. I'm not going to use them. If you want them, they're yours."

"No..." Dash insisted. "I'm okay."

I knew he would have loved to have the extra bars—he'd been rationing his—and I was fascinated to watch this play out. Dash-the-child would have gleefully accepted the food without a thought. Showing that kind of social awareness, unprompted by me, was another sign of his new maturity.

Jack could see it too. He glanced at me, and I grinned but didn't say anything, so Jack smiled and insisted. "Come on. I'll get them for you."

"Go ahead, Dash," I said, and that was all it took.

He followed Jack down to his tent and, about thirty minutes later, came back with an armful of various bars.

"He had, like, twenty bars!" Dash said. "I tried to only take one, but he made me take all these." He held forth half-a-dozen different Power Bars.

I'm pretty sure that's when Jack became Dash's favorite

trail friend. Later, whenever we would talk about people we'd met on the trail, Jack's name was always at the top of the list.

21

THE LONG WAIT

THE NEXT MORNING, we climbed that steep half-mile back to the trail with a spring in our step. Dash ate almost constantly, devouring Power Bar after Power Bar. It was like he'd been given the queen's own treasury.

We looked forward to the day's end, to our next Zero Day. Although this time, unlike our previous Zero Days, I didn't feel like I was going to be skidding across the finish line with a wrecked car, tires blown out and engine smoking, desperate for a rest. The Electric Blue Shoes had been flat-out amazing.

Lara and our daughter Elowyn were to pick us up at the end of Segment 17 which was, essentially, in the middle of nowhere at the side of Highway 114. The closest towns were Gunnison, thirty-nine miles to the west, and Saguache, thirty-one miles to the southeast. While we could have splurged on a hotel in Gunnison, we had decided it would be more cost effective to drive the hour back to the Buena Vista condo—which Chris and Carla had generously allowed us to use again—and rest up there.

The previous night, against all odds, I'd gotten a cell phone signal deep in the bowl of Baldy Lake. I'd talked to Lara and we'd made a plan to hit our meeting point at three-thirty in the afternoon the next day.

"But be sure to call me when you get there," she'd said. "I may need some guidance to find that stretch of highway."

"No problem," I'd said.

Unfortunately, last night was the last time I'd been able to capture a signal with my phone. I'd been sure once we got up the slope, the signal would be better than down in that bowl. It wasn't.

I swear, I don't know what mysterious force governs cell phone signals. It makes no sense. How I could get a signal in a literal bowl in the earth, surrounded by high ridges, but once we hiked to the top and got back on the trail, get zero bars? Can someone explain it to me?

We kept hiking and I kept watching the phone. After about three miles, I finally got a signal and called Lara.

"Hi honey," I said. "How's it going?"

"Uh..." She sounded distracted. "Hectic. There's a lot going on at work, and I'm trying to prep to get out the door."

"Gotcha. Well, I'll make this quick," I said. "We're making great time." We'd only had thirteen miles left on our final segment. We'd already burned up three of them, and it wasn't even ten o'clock yet. "We might get to the pick-up point an hour earlier than expected. Can you get us at two-thirty instead of three-thirty?"

"Um..." She hesitated. "Yeah. Okay. I'll aim for that. But let's sync up when you get there. I'll be there by three-thirty at the latest."

I told her that was no problem, and we hung up.

Dash picked a decent pace and we enjoyed the sunshine, the trees, and the many cows we'd begun to see on the flatter fields. Better yet, we hiked even faster than I'd anticipated. When one o'clock rolled around, we were only two miles from the end of the segment. That would put us at the pick-up spot around two o'clock.

I tried to call Lara. No bars. About one and a half miles

out, I tried again. No bars.

"How does that make sense?" I complained to Dash. "I can get a signal at freakin' Baldy Lake, but I can't get signal a mile from the highway?"

Dash just shrugged. I kept checking.

One mile out. No bars.

"Did you get her?" Dash asked.

"Can't," I said.

"Is she going to know where to pick us up?" he asked. His worry was justified. Some of the pick-up and drop-off points on The Colorado Trail were pretty obscure, and if one didn't know exactly where one was going, they'd be easy to miss.

"She's probably already there waiting for us," I said optimistically. "If not, we'll get a signal once we get to the highway."

We popped up onto Highway 114 at about two o'clock as predicted, and we saw a huge dirt parking lot just off the road with more than a half-dozen cars and two RVs.

"Well, she can hardly miss that," I said, feeling better.

"Oh cool," Dash said.

We had to walk a short stretch on the highway, and when we reached the parking lot, Jamil was there. He was jumping off the trail for a Zero Day in Gunnison and had already brokered a ride with a nice family who had just dropped off their college-aged kids at the trailhead.

My excitement became subdued when I discovered, even here on the highway, I had no signal. And Lara *wasn't* here already. No mini-van.

I asked Jamil if he could get a signal.

"Not on my cell," he said. "But I have a sat phone."

"That's handy," I said.

"Would you like to use it? It's pretty reliable. I can send a text from almost anywhere. The only thing that messes with it is cloud cover."

I looked overhead. Half the sky was blue, and half was obscured by slate gray clouds, bunching up for a typical afternoon rain shower.

He caught my glance and said, "It'll probably go through."

"Yes, please," I said.

"It costs a buck a text, though. So text her where you are, but ask her not to reply so I don't get an expensive back and forth."

"You got it." I offered to pay him for the text, but he waved that away.

I sent Lara a short description of the pick up point. I thanked Jamil, and he climbed into the truck and headed toward Gunnison.

Two-thirty came and went.

No Lara.

Oh well. She'd said she'd try to come earlier, but hadn't promised. And it had sounded like she was busy. But she said she'd make the three-thirty time at the very latest. We'd just have to chill out for an hour.

"I think we're going to have to wait until three-thirty, buddy," I said to Dash. He shrugged. We settled in to wait, plunking our packs down close to the gap in the barbed wire fence that marked the beginning of Segment 18.

We chatted with some of the other people coming and going, new hikers and the support crew dropping them off. We even saw Jack again. He was hiking with a young woman whose name escapes me—Rebecca or something—and she was determined to get another nine miles before sundown. We said brief hellos and goodbyes and watched them get smaller and smaller as they continued down the trail.

In celebration of it being our last day, we had already downed all of our food during the last couple of hours. I had one Clif Bar remaining, but I wasn't really hungry for another Clif Bar.

Then a trail angel approached. Her name was Mary, and she'd just dropped her daughter and a friend off at the trail. Mary had fresh oranges, and she offered them to us. After a week of living on Clif Bars, almonds, tuna packets, and freeze-dried food, those fresh oranges were like candy. We devoured everything she handed to us—three apiece, I think—and thanked her profusely before she left.

Three-thirty came and went.

"Where is she, Dad?" Dash asked.

"She'll be here, buddy. She's just running a little late. She had some stuff to do."

"Didn't she say she needed your help to find the place?"

"Yeah, but... We sent her that text on Jamil's phone."

"What if she didn't get it?" he asked.

"Well, she'll just have to find it on her own." Despite my casual tone, his comment mirrored my doubts. There were plenty of places to drive in Colorado that weren't here. For all I knew, Lara could be on the wrong highway, miles away.

We were also facing another problem. We'd timed our food and water with the notion that we weren't going to have to eat or refill. I only had a quarter liter of water left, and Dash was out. We were going to need to refill soon if Lara didn't get here.

Four o'clock came and went. No Lara.

"Dad?" Dash said.

"Yeah," I said. We were both getting antsy. Not only had Lara not reached us at the earlier pick-up time, but now she was half an hour late for our originally scheduled pick-up time.

Dash and I had both slipped into our city-life frame of mind, waiting for Lara, waiting to put up our feet and relax. Time to switch back to hiking-mind and take care of ourselves.

I checked the Data Book and, thankfully, there was a water source a tenth of a mile ahead. So we could get some water if we decided we needed it. That was a silver lining.

A number of cars had already passed us on the highway, but I hadn't been paying attention to them. I didn't *think* I'd noticed any Toyota mini-vans zip by, but I didn't know for sure. Also, I didn't figure Lara would miss this big parking lot, but I didn't know that for sure either. Maybe she had.

"Tell you what," I said. "Let's move our gear to edge of the road so she'll have a better chance of seeing us."

We moved our packs to where the barbed wire fence ended, just before the highway.

Something to note here. I often listen to my intuition. Or, at least, that's what I call those little mental nudges to do one thing over another. Or to *not* do something. Maybe there's no such thing as intuition, and what I'm sensing is just subconscious data that has collected in my brain pan and, while my conscious mind can't put it all together, my subconscious can, so it sends me signals encouraging me toward—or warning me against—a particular decision.

Or maybe it's just gut animal instinct, a kind of genetic magic that the rational mind can't comprehend. Whatever it is, I'd learned to lean on my intuition throughout my life, and I'd reaped great benefits from it.

All this to say: I was about to make the mistake of ignoring it.

Throughout our time on the trail, I'd watched Dash throw down his pack and flop on top of it when we'd stop to rest, using it like a big cushion. My intuition had told me not to do this myself. I mean, I had a stove, a Platypus, and an exposed sleeping pad in my kit, and I was a hundred pounds heavier than Dash. I didn't want to accidentally damage any of that vital equipment, so I never sat on my pack.

But right then, I was frustrated. I was hot. I was out of water. And I had hoped to get picked up an hour and a half ago, but now it was past four o'clock. There was nowhere to sit on this dusty gravel patch, and I just didn't care anymore. I dropped my pack and sat on top of it.

We watched cars go by. Once, there was a mini-van the same color as ours. I stood up and waved, but it drove past us, and the woman in the driver's seat didn't look much like Lara. But I'd only caught a glimpse of her profile for half a second as she'd whipped by at sixty miles per hour. Could it have been Lara? Had she missed the spot? I wasn't sure.

At four-fifteen, I hiked up a little dirt pile nearby to see if I could catch a cell signal. No dice.

Ten minutes later, I said, "Dash, I'm going to hike around the bend of the road—past that ridge—toward Gunnison, see if I get a signal."

He squinted in that direction.

"I figure it's half a mile," I said. "That'll take me fifteen minutes."

"I'll go with you," he said.

"No. Stay with the packs. I'll move faster if I don't have to carry my pack, and I don't want to just leave it by the side of the road. Besides, if Mom shows up, someone needs to be here."

"Okay."

I walked around the corner of the ridge. I even pushed farther than my allotted half mile, searching…searching…

Dammit! No signal. I wanted to keep going, but I couldn't see Dash anymore, and that bothered me. With a growl, I turned around and hiked back.

It was now after four-forty-five, and Dash was visibly nervous.

"What happened to her?" he asked.

"I'm sure she's fine," I said, but I wasn't actually sure. I tried not to let my nervousness spill over to Dash.

"Dad, maybe we should get a ride with someone," he said. "Get into town."

I was beginning to think he was right. After five o'clock, the traffic on the road was only going to decrease. The busy parking lot, once filled with more than a half-dozen cars and two RVs, was now empty.

Frustrated, I sat down hard on my pack and opened up my last Clif Bar. The road toward Gunnison was a bust, but the road toward Saguache went almost straight up to the top of a ridge. If there was a signal to be had, it would be at the top of that ridge. I could see the top from here, but that had to be a couple miles away and straight up. Almost an hour's trek.

"This sucks," I said, taking a bite of my Clif Bar. "We're going to have to filter some water soon." I contemplated the highway that climbed to that ridge in the distance. Maybe it would only be about half an hour to hike that…

But what if we still couldn't catch a signal at the top of it? Then what? There was no way we could just keep hiking and make it to Saguache. Not thirty-one miles. Our best day so far had been twenty miles, and that was hiking sunup to sundown. We wouldn't make it even ten miles before dark.

Well, I thought, *it would be better to take a shot at getting a signal at the top of the hill.*

That was really our only choice.

"I think I've got a plan, buddy," I said. "If we hike to the top of that ridge..." I trailed off as a heard a low hissing sound. I realized I'd been hearing it for a few seconds now, and it suddenly struck me that the hissing was coming from underneath me.

Snake? I thought for half a second.

No. I'd sat on my pack. I'd punctured my sleeping pad. Perfect. Just perfect.

I stood up and rolled my pack over, trying not to curse and spit that I'd just damaged my equipment when my intuition had *told* me not to fucking sit on my pack... But it wasn't my sleeping pad making the sound.

It was my can of bear mace.

When sleeping, I kept the bear mace by my feet in case I needed it. When hiking, I kept it in a quick-draw pouch on the side of my pack. After being jostled around and sat on, the can had half-rolled out of the quick-draw pouch and was trapped against the gravel. I thought for a split-second I'd punctured it. But it had stopped hissing when I'd stood up, and I saw the problem. The safety catch—a flat horseshoe of plastic that kept the trigger from being pushed—had turned sideways, allowing the trigger to be partially depressed. Which my weight had done. I'd been spraying a thin mist of bear mace into the dusty ground.

Gingerly, I picked up the can with both hands—one of which was still stupidly holding my half-a-Clif-Bar. I took a step away from Dash and pointed the spout toward the fence, away from us. I look back on that moment as the one smart thing I did.

The safety plastic had only come halfway off. It barely clung to the trigger, which more closely resembled a fire extinguisher than a firearm. Holding it at arm's length, I tried to push the askew piece of plastic back into place. It was wet, and my finger slipped.

A burst of bear mace shot out.

During my more idle moments of hiking the trail, I'd sometimes imagined fighting a bear with my bear mace. I'd imagined whipping out the can, flicking the safety plastic into the weeds, and shooting a straight stream of stinging nastiness into the bear's eyes.

But when the bear mace actually shot out, there was nothing straight about it. It was the equivalent of a sawed-off shotgun, blasting everything in front of me in a forceful, cone-shaped mist. I'd guess fifty percent went straight forward. The rest spewed out in a curling cloud left and right. The entire shot covered everything I could see, which thankfully only included dry gravel, tough thatches of shin-high grass, a barbed wire fence, and the drop-off to a gully beyond.

This shotgun effect was probably by design, I'd later reflect. After all, we aren't always as competent in real life as we are in our daydreams. Daydream Me, when encountering a bear, was cool and speedy and unerringly accurate, with the presence of mind to stand his ground, aim carefully, and fire.

But Real Life Me would probably panic at a charging bear, and if I did manage to bring the can of bear mace up in time, the accuracy of my shot would be highly suspect. It makes sense that bear mace would be designed to cover a swath of ground.

So maybe that cone-shaped spurt was by design. I don't know.

What I do know is: when you accidentally trigger bear mace for no reason, that shotgun design is pretty crappy. The blast went out, billowed left and right...

And curled right back into my eyes.

22

BEAR MACE TO THE FACE

"HOLY FUCK!" I cursed, dropping the can and the Clif Bar. Pain seared my eyes like someone had passed a welder's torch too close to them. Tears instantly streamed down my face. I went blind. I could only see blurry colors.

I instinctively raised my hands to rub at my eyes, to get the horrible stuff out, but I stopped, my fingers an inch away. My hands were wet with bear mace—they'd been on the leaky trigger.

"Dad!" Dash yelled. I could feel him near me, hovering, wanting to help, but I couldn't see him. I waved my hands in a warding-off gesture.

"Stay back. Get back!" I gasped, doubling over. My body felt electrified. My fists clenched. My back bowed. I wanted to get away from the pain, but there was no direction I could go.

I had to do something fast. God! It felt like someone was grinding glass into my eyes.

"I need water," I gasped, but even as I said it, I remembered I only had about three swallows left, somewhere tucked into my pack, which I could no longer see. And Dash had no water.

I thought of every bit of advice I'd ever been given as a child about what to do when something nasty gets into your eyes. Flush it out. Flush it away. Hold your head under a running faucet and let the water flow over your eye. Or, if you were in a high school chemistry lab, use that bottle flusher thing with the eye-shaped rubber thingy.

I had no bottle flusher. I had no faucet. My only water source was a tenth of a mile—and no less than fifteen minutes of water filtration—away. Aside from that, I had about three ounces in my Vapur.

My imagination went wild. If I didn't flush this out right now, could bear mace cause permanent blindness? Had I just blinded myself?

I'd skimmed the back of the bear mace package before ripping it open and seating the canister in its pouch. Blah blah blah, warnings and such about how you shouldn't spray yourself in the face. Duh. It had all been legalese cover-your-ass stuff, written only for the idiot who would actually do that. I'd only skimmed it—because what kind of idiot sprays bear mace into his own eyes?

Yeah.

Unfortunately, in my eye-rolling discounting of the back of the package, I'd skimmed over what I should do if I ended up being that idiot. And what the consequences would be.

I hunched over, wishing I could rub my eyes, while at the same time forcibly keeping my hands away from my face. My mind went in a dozen different directions.

I thought of useless platitudes like: would a spray that actually blinded bears be able to make it to the Costco shelves? It wouldn't do for hikers to go around blinding bears. Wouldn't animal rights activists have a fit? What about the FDA? They wouldn't approve a product like that, right? Just in case some idiot like myself sprayed himself in the eyes? That could hardly be legal.

I felt Dash's touch on my arm and I flinched. He grabbed my hand and pressed my nearly-empty Vapur bottle into it.

"Did it get you?" I said. "Are you okay?"

"It didn't hit me. I'm fine." His voice was worried. "But what about you? What do we do?"

"Just give me a second." I didn't know how I was going to be able to flush my eyes if I couldn't see. I mean, even if I had a gallon of water, most of it would probably miss before I got a good flush. With this small amount, I had to be careful. I had to be accurate.

Blinking furiously, I realized the pain had begun to recede.

My panic decreased with it. It couldn't have been more than a minute since that cloud had hit my eyes. If the pain was already going, that had to be a good sign, right? Maybe I wasn't going to go blind after all.

I blinked, trying to clear my vision, and I could make out a few things. The fence. The lump of my pack, the chalky gravel beneath my feet.

"I think it's getting better," I said.

"I'm going to filter some water," Dash said, pulling open my pack and rummaging around for the Platypus. "I'll run to the stream."

I went over and sat down on my pack, no longer caring about anything being punctured or destroyed. My left eye was better than my right, and details were starting to reappear. I could kind of see now. I saw Dash bolt through the gap in the fence and run down the trail.

I leaned my head to the side, making sure my hands didn't come anywhere near the spout of my Vapur, and gently dribbled water over my eyes. The result was wonderful. The stinging, though still present, went down immediately. But more importantly, my *I'm going to go blind* panic subsided. I could mostly see now. Rather than just big blobs of color, it was more like I'd gotten dust in my eyes and, while it was painful to open them, at least they were operating like normal, very watery, eyes.

By the time Dash returned with the extra water, I actually didn't feel I needed it anymore. But at his insistence, I flushed my eyes again anyway.

"Well," I said at last. "That could have been worse."

He laughed and shook his head.

Before washing my hands, I went back to the dropped can. Part of me wanted to pick it up and huck it into the gully. Instead, I faced my newly born fear of bear mace and completed what I'd tried to do before, this time far more carefully. I set the safety clip back in place and rinsed off the bottle and my hands, then set the can next to my pack.

It was now five-twenty-five, and still no Lara. She was almost two hours late. I picked up my dirt-dusted, half-eaten Clif Bar and sniffed it. It smelled like bear mace. Great. I wrapped it up and tucked it in the Ziploc bag I carried to store trash.

"What the hell happened to her?" I murmured. I began to worry for other reasons. Visions of car crashes rose in my mind.

"We have to do something, Dad. We can't just sit here."

"Yeah," I said.

"We need to hitchhike," he said.

No, I thought. *We are absolutely not hitchhiking.*

First of all, while I had hitchhiked prodigiously in my youth, I felt pretty damned iffy hitchhiking with a child. I applaud adults who run ridiculous risks for good reasons. Or sometimes even whimsical reasons. But I didn't like the idea of putting my son in that questionable position. Not when there were other options.

I also felt embarrassed about not having thought of this possibility and having no plan to get us out of it. I mean, sure, we couldn't control when Lara got here. That part was out of our hands. But I could have planned the food thing better. If I'd held even a bit of food in reserve, we could have pitched the tent and waited until morning.

I was embarrassed at my poor planning, and even more embarrassed that I'd just bear-maced myself. I absolutely did not want to meet new people right now. I definitely didn't want to beg a ride from one.

I stood up and looked at the ridge to the south. The

highway snaked up to it and over. That was our next move. We'd just strap up and continue to the top of that hill. Surely there'd be a signal.

Except while I'd told *myself* we weren't hitchhiking, I had neglected to tell Dash.

I turned to find him practically standing in the middle of the highway. An extra cab truck hauling a flatbed trailer with an old Ford Bronco strapped to it bore down on him.

I sucked in a lungful of air to shout at him, tell him to get the hell out of the road, when the truck pulled into the parking lot. Dash grinned and ran toward me.

"Got us a ride!" he said.

I wanted to tell him that, no, we weren't hitchhiking... But the guy had already pulled over.

I guess we're doing this, I thought. My plan of hiking to the top of that ridge vanished. Okay, a five-minute car ride was better than a forty-minute hike.

I hopped over the hitch between the truck and the trailer and went to the driver's side window. My fears eased as I noticed the driver's wife was in the passenger's seat, and there were three kids in the extra cab. I immediately felt better. I'd have felt far more sketchy about someone driving alone. A guy with his family seemed okay. He had an open, friendly face.

"What's up, my friend?" he said with a light Latino accent. His wife peered at me from behind him, no expression at all.

"Thanks for stopping," I said. "Our ride didn't show up, and I was wondering if you can get cell service on your phone. If I could just call her, I could find out what we're looking at."

He pulled out his phone, tapped at it a couple of times, then shook his head. "I'm sorry, my friend. I got no service."

Chagrined, I nodded. I had hoped maybe it was just my provider. Dang. But I kept an upbeat tone. "Hey, would you mind giving me and my son a ride to the top of that hill?" I pointed.

He glanced at the ridge in the distance, then at his wife, then back at me. "Just to the top of the hill?"

"Yeah. I should be able to get a signal up there."

"No problem, my friend. Hop in back."

"Thank you so much. You're a lifesaver."

Dash and I grabbed our packs and piled into the cluttered back of the truck. There was a spare tire, various tools, a couple of coolers, and a myriad of other things I can't remember. We wedged ourselves in, and I did a quick pat and a last-minute double-check of the gravel parking lot to make sure we hadn't left anything behind.

Then we were off, crouched amid the clutter and clutching our packs. The wind whipped at us. I tucked my ball cap under my butt to make sure it didn't fly away.

I looked toward the top of the ridge like it was our salvation, but when we got there...

No service.

The driver slowed, but didn't stop. He held up his phone, looked over his shoulder through the cab's back window past the heads of his three children, and asked with a glance, "Did you get service?"

I shook my head, sure that if we went a little further, a bar or two would jump up on my phone. He seemed to read my mind and pointed further down the road. I nodded. He drove on. We were now angling downhill, and the parking lot, the trailhead, everything that connected us to the CT, vanished behind us. All around were beautiful sandstone formations and the highway in front of us.

I huddled against the wind, and my imagination ran wild. I thought of all the horrible parenting moves I was making in this one moment. Trusting our lives to someone I didn't know. Sitting in the back of a truck bed that barely had enough room for us and our gear, let alone seat belts. And we were barreling down the highway at sixty miles per hour.

I hadn't had a contingency plan for if we didn't get picked up. I'd bear-maced myself. And now I was putting my son's life at risk. I was the worst dad ever.

I glanced over at Dash. His head was up, his mane of sandy hair streaming out behind him, and he was grinning like a dog with his head out the window.

"This is the best," he shouted over the rushing air. "This is the best part of the trip so far!"

My self-recrimination melted away, and I laughed. "What?" I shouted back.

"This!" He gestured with his hands. His left got caught by the wind and whipped back before he tucked it against his chest. "Who gets to do this?"

He turned my entire mood around. He was right. We weren't dead yet, and what was adventure without risk? This was, in a way, the reason we'd come to do the trail in the first place. Not hitchhiking, of course, but for him to experience things he hadn't experienced before.

"You're right," I shouted back, letting my dark thoughts go. He continued looking forward, and then his head suddenly whipped to the side as some cars flashed by us.

"Hey, I just saw a mini-van," he said, spinning back to look at me.

I craned my neck, trying to follow the line of three cars that were already as small as toys in the distance. I couldn't get a fix on the one in the lead, but it could have been a mini-van.

"Was it Mom?" I asked.

"I don't know." He held up his hands. "It went by too fast."

I checked my phone, hoping there would finally be a signal. I mean, we had cleared the ridge. We were miles down the road.

Still nothing.

My lifted spirits deflated. It was impossible to know if that van was Lara.

My foreboding grew as the truck slowed and finally pulled over to the side of the road next to a sagebrush desert with those beautiful stony formations in the distance.

I was sure the driver was done hauling us up the road. We'd asked to be taken to the top of the ridge, and he'd already taken us miles past that.

Now, as the truck trundled to a stop and leaned a little sideways from the slope of the shoulder, I realized we were in an entirely new fix. We were now in the middle of nowhere with no trail, no map indicating local water sources, and no way to contact Lara. If he dropped us off here, it was going to be a long trek backward to Square One. We'd come at least five miles already. Maybe ten.

The driver hopped out of the cab, and I waited for the axe to fall, waited for him to say, "Okay man, you've got to get out. I took you much farther than I promised already."

Instead, he said, "Sorry, my friend. The brakes are overheating from this downhill." He pointed back the way we'd come. "And there's another big downhill coming up. I have to let them cool down before I go."

"Oh, that's no problem," I said, daring to be hopeful.

"Are you thirsty?" he asked, handing me and Dash a couple bottles of Vitamin Water he already had in his hands. "You must be thirsty."

"Wow, thanks," I said. Dash cracked open the bottle and drank it immediately.

The man looked up the road speculatively, then back at me. "It'll just be a minute. You know, we're going all the way to Saguache. We could take you there."

"Really?"

"Sure, my friend."

It took me about a millisecond to make that decision. I mean, I'd wanted to grab a signal and call Lara. That had been my primary goal. But that hadn't worked, and now we were on a flat, still with no signal, and I wasn't confident I was going to get one anytime soon. I'd just assumed there'd have to be one after a few miles. Dead zones along the I-25 corridor—which was primarily what I drove these days—didn't exist anymore.

But even if I did get a signal sooner than Saguache, there was no guarantee that Lara—who might have been in that van that whipped by us and would now be in the middle of the dead zone—would be able to answer me.

So...yes. I did want to go to Saguache. It was far preferable to walking by the side of the road in the middle of nowhere. And if that *had* been Lara who'd passed us, she'd have to come back through Saguache to get to Buena Vista. It was a strategically sound choice all the way around.

"That would be amazing," I said as all of that mental chatter flew through my mind.

"If you would like to ride in the Bronco, you can do that," he said. "Instead of the back of the truck."

"Um…sure," I said.

So Dash and I actually climbed into the old Ford Bronco strapped to the trailer and rode there instead. About five minutes from Saguache, I finally got cell service and texted Lara. Yes, they'd been in the Toyota mini-van Dash had seen. I told her where we'd be in Saguache, and she said they were coming to get us.

We stopped at the first gas station in town, and Dash and I piled out of the Bronco. We finally did official introductions with Sergio, Letty, and their kids.

They were from Center, Colorado, and they were the most generous people in the world. We talked for a while. I thanked them profusely for saving us, and we exchanged information. When Sergio discovered I was a fantasy novelist, he mentioned that his daughter loved reading fantasy.

"Well, any books I've written are free for you. Take a look at my website and choose any or all that you'd like. I'll send them to you."

"And will you sign them?" Sergio asked.

"Of course. The works."

Weeks later, when Dash and I had finished the trail and were back in Denver, I would make a pilgrimage down to Center with a stack of my books to surprise Sergio and his family. I signed a book for each of his kids, and for him and for his wife, Letty. My intention was to give some small recompense for the huge favor they did us, but I ended up getting far more out of the bargain than they did. Not only did they feed me the most amazing Mexican food I'd ever eaten—and they just kept the courses coming one after the other—but I got to see the inner workings of their restaurant, meet their parents, and watch Letty's father make restaurant-style refried beans. I am a fiend for good refried beans, and seeing the entire process was richly rewarding.

By the time they were done feeding me, they had to roll me out the door because I was wider than I was tall. And on top of it all, they sent me home with dinner for the whole family.

Our hitchhiking adventure not only saved us from an uncomfortable situation, but it opened up a whole new friendship. I kept thinking back about how right Dash had been, leaning into the wind with his hair streaming behind him, despite all of my parental misgivings.

Eventually, we said goodbye to Sergio and Letty, promised to keep in touch, and settled down to eat some junk food outside the gas station convenience store.

By the time Lara rolled up, Dash and I were feasting on Pringles, M&Ms, Reese's Peanut Butter Cups and fountain Cokes.

Turns out Lara had sent me a string of texts letting me know they had gotten a late start out of Denver, that the drive from Buena Vista had been much longer than anticipated, and that they were going to be late...

...and of course, I'd received none of those texts.

If Dash and I had waited fifteen minutes more—just fifteen minutes!—there would have been no need to panic. There would have been no hitchhiking. No trip to Saguache.

On the other hand, we'd never have met Sergio and his family, and my life would be the poorer for it.

23

RIVER SIRENS

DASH AND I were ready for another amazing Zero Day in Buena Vista. But this time was different. Elo had joined the party, and I wasn't laid up with ravaged-foot syndrome.

Calluses had developed on the previously troubled spots. I'd picked up a few new blisters on the tips of my toes because of my brand new shoes. But those blisters were laughable. After enduring the inch-and-a-half diameter blisters on the balls of my feet and heels, these tiny new ones didn't even rate on the pain-o-meter. I taped them up and barely thought of them.

We watched movies. We chatted with Elo and Lara. We went to dinner. I ate a freakin' pound of M&Ms. And not once did Dash mention not wanting to continue. I was happy to find that I'd called that correctly.

In fact, he did all of his gear unpack, clean-up, and repack himself. Like me, he could see the finish line now. We had hiked for three weeks. We only had two to go.

Also, the coming legs of the journey were relatively shorter than the first three. The next leg would take us to Lake City—

only four days away rather than seven.

After that, we would head into the high-high-country, but only for three days before reaching our final stopover at Molas Pass, where we'd resupply and pick up Raeden for the final six-day hike into Durango.

In short, after doing the seven-days-at-a-time pace for the first three weeks, the last two weeks were going to be a piece of cake. Sure, there were challenges. The altitude was going to climb significantly. There was going to be a twenty-mile dry stretch where we'd have to haul the drom with a few gallons of water, but we were conditioned now. We were excited.

After a lovely rest, we left Buena Vista so early that Elo just mumbled, "G'bye" from her bed. Lara drove us back to the Segment 18 trailhead, right where I'd bear-maced myself.

We snapped selfies as the sun rose behind us, and said our goodbyes. We wouldn't see Lara or Elo for another two weeks, not until we crossed the finish line in Durango.

I felt good, physically. My fifty-year-old body had done me right, adapting and rising to this challenge. I anticipated less "gutting it out" this time and more enjoyment of the wild.

I also felt good spiritually. Our hitchhiking adventure and the helpful hikers along the way had reinforced for me that people are basically good. I hadn't looked at strangers that way in a long time. In the city, I'd been trapped in my own social echo chamber where there's so much discussion of "us" versus "them." In that soup, it's so hard to ignore the rants on social media that brew hateful rhetoric. But out in the wilderness, everything we experienced was first-hand. We didn't see the world through the skewed lens of social media, which seemed to breed fears and hate built on second-hand, third-hand, or fourth-hand information. I hadn't realized how much time I'd spent trying to decide what was real and what was lies. And to think the world actually operated that way, that people in general were angrier, ready to fight. It was easy to believe that all that vitriol crammed at us every minute of the day, demanding attention and credibility, was actually a fair reflection of reality.

On the trail, there was no second-guessing what was real. There was no nail-biting uncertainty about what deserved attention and what didn't. I didn't need an expert from some Reddit post to tell me that we shouldn't summit a ridge in the afternoon while the skies were clouding up. I didn't need an "influencer" to tell me I needed to refill water at this spot, not the next one. There was no question about the truth. It was right in front of me all the time. I could trust the input because it wasn't based on opinion. It was just...real.

I loved the simplicity of it. I was officially more comfortable in a strange stretch of woods I'd never seen before than a new town I'd never seen before. I could rely on the natural rhythm of the wilderness. I'd even come to rely on the character of the average hiker. Open. Friendly. Generous.

But city folk weren't predictable. I'd had years of experience determining that. I put up emotional barriers in a town, while I took them down in the wild.

And lordy, I'd forgotten how much energy those emotional barriers spent. On the trail, I didn't feel mentally exhausted all the time. In a very real way, the CT made me younger.

So we started out Segment 18 with a smile. Dash and I calculated everything now. Who had what food and how much it weighed. Distance to the next water source. Where we'd eat lunch. Where we were planning to bed down for the night. The elevation gain and loss. Everything. And at the same time, we were both open to changing the plan depending on what the land threw at us.

At this point, we lived by both the Data Book and an app that Fleet had introduced called Guthook. We leaned on the Data Book to plan and on Guthook to give us up-to-the-minute information about water sources.

Segment 18 was just shy of fourteen miles, and my feet felt fantastic, nearly pre-CT normal. Not only that, but there were no tall mountains for the next two sections.

"I'm thinking it's a twenty-mile day," I said to Dash.

"Duh," he said.

I laughed. "Feeling cocky, are you?" I asked.

"It's totally flat, Dad. We can hit twenty."

"Let's prove it."

We leaned into it and got to work, kicking up our pace across the long flat fields. We were in the midst of cow land again. We spotted cow patties, though we hadn't yet spotted actual cows. We joked and talked. A couple miles into the trail we found an amazing stand of aspens with an old, scarred grandfather aspen in the center. We spent a moment there, just appreciating the grandeur of it and snapping pictures.

We tested our trust in the Platypus that day, too. We'd planned to refill our Vapurs at a little creek up ahead, but when we got to it, all we found was a little trickle with a million zillion cow hooves stamped into the muddy bank.

"Uh... Yuck," Dash said.

"Three parts water. Two parts cow crap," I agreed dubiously.

Unfortunately, there wasn't another water source for miles, and our Vapurs were nearly empty. After a long time staring at the thing, we swallowed our trepidation, found the cleanest-looking part of the creek and worked that water filter.

I confess that I waited for giardia to strike. It was in the back of my mind over the next couple of days. But it never did.

After filling up, Dash decided we needed new trail names. I'd started out as "Epic" and I'd dubbed Dash "Camel" because of his inhuman ability to stretch his water resources. But he wasn't sure he liked that trail name, and he was certain he didn't like mine.

"What's wrong with Epic?" I asked.

"It's too..." he said. "I don't know. It's too complimentary."

"Hey, I like complimentary."

"Come on. A trail name needs to be a little self-deprecating, based on some habit you have, or an event that's unique to the trail. Something like that."

"Epic is based on a habit I have."

"Come on, Dad."

"Self-deprecating, huh?"

"Goofy is better."

We spent the day brainstorming trail names. After a few hours of kicking around possibilities, we'd hammered them down. Due to Dash's incessant habit of squirreling away wrappers in all of his various pouches and then forgetting to empty them when it came time to hang the bear bag, I dubbed him Packrat.

In a flash of genius, Dash drew my new trail name from the animated movie *Bolt,* one of his favorite movies as a kid. There's a scene in which a hapless dog shelter employee gets pepper-sprayed in the face while Bolt and Rhino the hamster spring Mittens from her cage. The employee falls down, wipes frantically at his face and shouts, "Awww! Spicy eyes!"

"That's it!" Dash exclaimed. "You're Spicy Eyes."

I laughed. We kept it. My name was now Spicy Eyes.

Satisfied, Dash ranged out ahead and we kept going for that twenty-mile day.

During an afternoon rainstorm, we passed the three-hundred-mile mark, which went uncelebrated as we were both concentrating on staying dry. But I'd been paying attention. Hunched down into the hood of my rain jacket, I quietly smiled as we moved past that milestone. Three hundred. Wow. That was like walking all the way across the state of Pennsylvania, except with mountains.

When we stopped for lunch during a break in the clouds, I told Dash about crossing the three-hundred-mile mark.

His low-key response matched its lack of fanfare.

He just shrugged and kept eating. That made me feel good, though. He wasn't focused on the miles. He was just enjoying the trail. The two-hundred-mile threshold had been a big deal. The one-hundred-mile threshold before that had been an even bigger deal. But this time, it was just business as usual.

That was more profound than a celebration, I realized. The miles didn't matter anymore. The next adventure did, the next discovery of what The Colorado Trail could show us.

After we finished lunch, he was game to take a picture to

celebrate our three-hundred-mile mark, though he kept making goofy faces at the camera.

As we passed the twenty-two-mile mark for the day, Dash was pretty spent. We reached the Cochetopa River, which was where we'd planned to camp, but none of the campsites appealed. And after such a long day, I thought we deserved a really good campsite, worthy of our longest day yet, so I pressed on.

Dash lagged behind me, which was a rarity. He was fragged out, but I was invigorated by my happy feet and last night's good rest. I kept pushing toward a stand of trees ahead.

I far preferred to camp within a stand of trees to out in the open. Maybe it was some kind of residual fear left over from Searle Pass, but I felt safer in the forest, especially at night. I liked how quiet it was, how close. I felt protected.

Unfortunately, that stand of trees ahead ended up being a bust. No good campsite there. The ground wasn't flat and the river was a distant slog through marsh and tall weeds. We pushed on.

The trail wound uphill into some aspens, which had amazing flat sites. Someone had already put up their tent in one of them...

But the river was half a mile away.

I wanted to see what was next, what was closer to the river. The eternal optimist in me just knew there'd be a perfect campsite.

This time, I was right.

We descended a steep slope to a fantastic flat field at the edge of a drop-off to the river. On one side of the drop-off, a trail wended down, as pretty as you please.

"This looks awesome," I said. "Let's go down to the river, get some water, then come back here."

Dash looked wilted. Twenty-four miles of hiking in the sun had finally done us both in. We were hot, sweaty, and thirsty. All I wanted to do was drop tent, stuff face, and crash.

As we descended the trail, I realized the tall weeds by the river weren't weeds at all. They were some odd cross between trees and bushes. I couldn't actually label them. They were short, leafy, many-limbed trees, barely taller than I was. Hundreds of hikers over the years had beaten a number of trails through them, and there didn't seem to be any rhyme or reason to the paths. It was like walking into a hedge maze.

I was instantly charmed.

"Let's see if we can find the water," I said.

Dash, rejuvenated by the new adventure, dove eagerly into the maze and vanished from view. I wound my way through, actually having to backtrack once. I finally found something that looked like a main path, and I heard Dash's voice ahead, speaking in conversational tones. He'd found someone.

I could hear the rush of the water. I knew I was close even though I still couldn't see the river, so I found a small break in the wall of tree-bushes and dropped my pack, pulled out the Platypus and headed toward the sound. I broke through the foliage to find Dash standing at the beginning of a log bridge that went halfway across the river before sinking beneath the waterline. He was talking with two college-aged women who were frolicking in the current.

We'd passed them earlier that day while they were having lunch, and then they'd passed us while we were having lunch. We'd exchanged enough short pleasantries to say hello and catch their names: Paige and Bree.

Paige, bespectacled and serene, sat on the log bridge right where it began to sink beneath the water, her legs in the current. Bree was floating face-up in the calmer pool created by the log bridge. She sat up when she saw me, then stood up in the shallow water, her shorts and jog bra completely soaked.

"Come on in," she said brightly. "The water's amazing."

The whole scene made me grin. If I'd been their age, I'd have dived in without thinking, dry clothes be damned. But at age fifty, I tended to think a few steps ahead. The sun was already low in the sky. The air was warm, but in about thirty minutes it was going to be cool. In an hour, it was going to be cold.

I laughed. "Maybe next time."

"Suit yourself." She fell back into the water, submerging again.

"Hey," I said. "Are you camping up there?" I pointed back the way we'd come. "On the flat space up the cliff?"

Paige nodded. "Sure enough."

"Would you mind if my son and I grabbed a spot up there with you?"

Bree came up again, standing and raising her arms with a smile. "We don't own the wilderness. Camp wherever you want."

Her bright spirit was infectious. "Thank you," I said, and I set about filtering a few gallons of water while Dash continued talking with them. Bree got out just a few minutes later, dried off, and Dash went with both of them up to the campsite.

I finished up and followed soon after. Dash and I respectfully waited and let them choose their site first before we put down our tent. We also invited them to share what we were cooking, and we had a nice little dinner together. We all munched and fell to talking.

Bree had just graduated from college, and she was interested in going into fashion. Paige, who was constantly writing in her journal, told us she was a grad student and that she was meeting her boyfriend at the end of the next segment.

We regaled them with stories from the trail, told them about our trail names. Bree was amused by my trail name and asked me how I came by it. I told her the Bear Mace to the Face story. Both she and Paige laughed at that.

"You know," Bree said. "I knew this girl who went to hike The Colorado Trail with a group of her friends, and she had a bear mace incident, too."

"Do tell," I said.

"So..." She shook her head with a smile. "She and her friends head onto the trail, hike all day, and then they set up their first campsite, right? She takes out her bear mace and walks around the camp, using it like bug spray. Spraying everything and everyone."

"No!" I said.

"She did!" Bree chuckled. "Sprayed the whole campsite. Everyone went to the hospital. Ended their trip just like that."

Dash and I laughed. We all fell to eating, polishing off the final remainders of both pots of food. We also gave them some of the homemade brownies Elo had baked for us. Paige and Bree were ecstatic. Any kind of baked goods were a rarity on the trail, and Elowyn's baking is divine.

"So, you didn't give us your trail names," I said. "You know ours. What are yours?"

"We don't do trail names," Paige said.

"Oh?" I said. "Why not?"

She shrugged. "I don't know. It seems a little like there's an elitism to it. Like there are 'real-hikers' who have trail names and 'not-real-hikers' who don't."

"Huh," I said, turning that over in my mind. I hadn't thought about it that way at all. Like Dash, I'd pretty much viewed trail names as a fun game to play while we were out here, not as a way to join some secret club. I hadn't gotten that impression from other people I'd met with trail names, either. But then, I loved nicknames.

We finished our meals and hung our bear bags. I helped Paige, as two people hanging a bear bag is way easier than one. Then we all retired to our tents and conked out.

I woke up at about three in the morning to attend the call of nature, and afterwards took pictures of the glorious moon in the night sky. I don't know what it is, but the moon out in the wilderness is bigger, brighter. The light is so bright it drives back the darkness all around. I took pictures until I began to shiver, then I ran back to the tent.

The next morning, Paige was already gone by the time we got up. Turns out that Paige and Bree weren't actually hiking together in any long-term sense. They'd just met up on the trail and decided to team up for a while.

Bree was already up. She struck camp, said a sunny goodbye to both of us, and left while we were eating our morning oatmeal.

Sunny, cloudless skies followed us as we got back on the

trail, making it a joy to see this deep, backwoods country. We climbed steadily higher over the course of the next few days, popping above the tree line here and there, though always timing it before noon or after three o'clock. As a result, we had no problems with weather. Ah, wisdom.

One of my favorite campsites had a beaver dam, a beaver swimming about in the lake and…a moose! We watched that moose for the better part of an hour, pulling in hikers who were about to pass by and letting them know about it. By the time the moose finally ambled up the far slope on the other side of the lake, we had become friends with a trio of hikers—Candyman, Hot Mess, and Seeker—and we swapped stories for long after the moose left.

I confess I felt uneasy putting our tent down in moose territory, but the big guy was all the way across the lake, and I figured he was unlikely to make a nighttime sneak-attack on our tent. My understanding of moose is that they don't care about you unless you get between them and their water source, or if you antagonize them.

A friend of mine who worked in Alaska told me about a co-worker who decided one drunken evening to throw snowballs at a moose. The fifteen-hundred-pound beast made a *gronk* sound, ran over, knocked the guy down, and punched a few hoof-shaped holes in his chest.

My friend had said that was an example of natural selection at work. Some people just didn't use the brains they were born with.

So apparently, when it comes to black bears, yell and scream and spook them. They'll go away. When it comes to moose, don't do that. Don't give them a reason to look your direction at all.

The moose never bothered us, but our perfect campsite ended up less-than-perfect for another reason: I had a crazy allergy attack.

Typically, I don't have strong allergies. But some mutant flower must have been blooming near that lake—and not *anywhere* else on The Colorado Trail—because my nose hated it. By the time we hung the bear bag and settled down in the tent, my nose was Niagara Falls. I used up almost our whole roll of toilet paper.

That was also the night a fiendish bug landed on the tent, right above our faces, as we settled into our sleeping bags in the dying light. The high country isn't known for giant bugs, but this guy was a monster. It was the size of Dash's face, and it made us jump when it landed on the bug netting. We watched in fascination—snapping pictures and being frightfully glad we were in the tent—until it flew away. Dash called it the Mosquito Tarantula Hawk Wasp.

Thankfully, my exploding nose and the Mosquito Tarantula Hawk Wasp were the only events of note. We rose early in the morning and actually got onto the trail by seven o'clock. The next day we chilled out a bit, slowing our pace and tacking on an easy fourteen-miler after our monster twenty-three-point-eight-mile day.

That night, we rolled into a campsite in the shadow of San Luis Peak, right at the edge of the tree line. There was only one tall tree within sight. The rest were the stunted, ten-foot tall pines I'd come to associate with this elevation, plus lots of those tree-bushes that had been clustered around the Cochetopa River.

I was apprehensive, not just because of having to camp out in the open after our Searle Pass excursion, but because the only place to hang a bear bag was that single tall tree. It was the right height, had one long stout limb over ten feet up, and was over two hundred feet from our campsite. It was perfect, and yet...

There was something wrong with that tree.

It was dark and gnarled and angry, something from a horror movie, a hangman's tree.

As we set up our tent that evening down the slope, under the distant, sullen gaze of that tree, it spooked the hell out of me. No matter where I was or what I was doing—setting up the tent, making dinner, digging a latrine—I was aware of it. It unlocked my imagination, and I entertained all kinds of creepy

Legend of Sleepy Hollow stories surrounding the angry tree.

I imagined an undead bear wandering the highlands, gobbets of rotting flesh falling from its bony carcass as it lumbered along the slopes, a slave to the malevolent sentience within the tree. The bear waited for unsuspecting hikers who dared spend the night under the tree's baleful gaze, then lumbered down the hill to kill them....

I imagined red-eyed ravens watching from within the dark hollows of the tree, letting hiker after hiker pass in the daytime, but if someone had the gall to stop when night fell, to pitch their tent nearby, the red-eyed ravens would ensure those arrogant fools never woke up again.

By the time the sun had gone down and I marched up the slope to the Malevolent Tree, I didn't want to hang my bear bag on it anymore. Such disrespect couldn't possibly be forgiven. The undead bear would come charging down the slope. The red-eyed ravens would shoot out of the hollows in a swarm, ripping the flesh from my bones—

"Oh just get it done," I muttered to myself, but my hands shook as I quickly tied the rock, threw the line, and hoisted the bag. When I was done, I swallowed, whipped out my phone and took a picture of the creepy-ass tree.

Then I turned and scrambled down that slope in the dark much faster than I should have.

Of course, the picture didn't turn out. All I caught was the moon in the sky and a few crooked branches like thin fingers reaching toward the light. I didn't share any of my internal spooky stories with Dash.

It rained that whole night. I slept fitfully, my dreams filled with bears and ravens. At least there was no thunder.

We woke in the morning alive and unharmed, and the sunrise was the most beautiful I'd ever seen. I took a panorama of the moon on one side of us and the rising sun on the other.

We had forced ourselves to get up super early because we wanted to take a crack at bagging a peak that was off-trail. San Luis is one of the more remote 14'ers in Colorado, and its peak was only a one-and-a-half-mile deviation from The Colorado

Trail.

After a steep hike, Dash and I reached the saddle and a fork in the trail. The Colorado Trail turned downhill to the left, but the other path veered right, leading eventually to the top of San Luis Peak. We dropped our packs and took the detour. After all, it was only a mile and a half.

But let me tell you something about that last thousand feet of elevation up a 14'er. It's like hiking on a different planet. I mentioned before that trees vanish from the slopes at about eleven thousand three hundred feet. Above thirteen thousand feet, all other life vanishes as well. It's just cliff faces and jumbled slopes of rock. The only living thing I saw was lichen. And that sucker was only on one rock. Out of millions. There's not even dirt up there. The only way to mark the trail was by making cairns of loose stones.

Oh, and the air vanishes, too.

Dash and I sucked wind, our legs seemed to lose strength, and the temperature vacillated wildly. One minute, we were sweating in the sun. The next minute, an icy wind cut through us and we huddled into our puffer jackets. 14'ers are intense.

But we bagged the summit, took beautiful shots of the vista, and headed back down. On the way up, Dash had noticed I'd deviated from the trail a couple times, picking my own route over the jagged rocks. On the way down, he scolded me.

"Dad, you're not as agile as you were in your twenties, so don't do anything stupid. See that one cliff over there? You didn't seem to even notice it on the way up. You just walked right up to that edge, and you scared the hell out of me. If you stumble, you're dead. You'll just fall right off and die. So don't mess around."

It amused me to see him treat me like he needed to protect me, just as I'd done for him so many times.

But his advice was well-taken. I watched my step going down.

We got back on the trail without me falling to my death, and we enjoyed the rest of the sunny day. That afternoon, as we descended toward Lake City, my buddy A.J. from Texas met up with us. He'd hiked in a few miles just to spend some time on the trail with us. It was amazing to see him, and not only did he bring us fresh apricots and pastries, he shared his own fresh-made turkey sandwich.

We devoured everything, and he laughed happily as we did so.

As we hiked back over the territory A.J. had covered on his way in, Dash ranged ahead, and A.J. and I reminisced about our time in school together, from elementary school to high school. We talked about camping when we were in second grade. We talked about elementary school crushes and high school crushes and basically had a blast with the past.

We reached his car late that afternoon. Dash and I flopped into the comfort of form-fitting seats while A.J. drove us into Lake City. That night, we stayed at The Texan, a cool, quirky little waystation for travelers of all kinds. It was too eclectic to call it a motel, with its mismatched cabins and asymmetrical buildings, but it was the perfect place to rest one's feet, chat with one's childhood chum, and—of course—devour cheeseburgers and fries from Packer Saloon & Cannibal Grill. With a name like that, the revivified adventurer in me just had to bite. And let me tell you...the burgers were delectable.

And I wondered if I should be just a little scared about that...

Happily chomping away and ensconced at The Texan, we discovered one downside to our cozy, quirky overnight cabin: the wifi sucked! I was eager to continue telling our journey on Facebook, and I had finished up the latest post a couple of hours before midnight when...

The wifi failed. The page re-set. And I lost all of it.

I rewrote it, posted it again. Wi-fi fail. Lost it again. Posted it again. Wi-fi fail. Grrr...

With Dash and A.J. both fast asleep, I silently cursed and spat that I was losing precious sleeping time—in a real bed, no less! But I kept at it. I came at it from a half-dozen different directions until finally, around midnight, I managed to get the thing posted.

I practically threw my phone onto the nightstand and crashed hard.

The next morning, we stopped at a cute little cafe-and-mountain-bike-shop called Confluence and grabbed three breakfast burritos. We wolfed them down as A.J. drove us back to the Segment 22 trailhead...

Where we were greeted by an unexpected surprise. A group of trail angels had set up on the north side of the trail with a canopy for shade and a smorgasbord of food.

Trail angels are individuals—or groups of people—who take time out of their summer to drive up to a trailhead and give away food. These angels might be previous hikers, they might be part of someone's support crew, or they might just be people who like to do nice things. Wherever they come from, catching a glimpse of a trail angel is like catching a glimpse of a rainbow, complete with the pot of gold at the end. Trail angels bring donuts. They bring soft drinks. Sandwiches. Cookies. Candy. Anything and everything a hiker might crave—but typically wouldn't carry—on the trail.

Trail angels are *wonderful*.

And this group had really done a job. Many trail angels bring easily-handled items, like what I mentioned above. This group had set up three grills and were rocking a full-on pancake breakfast, complete with sausage and bacon. Not only that, but they also had fresh fruit, cookies, and donuts. A dozen other hikers were clustered about, taking advantage of their amazing generosity. The angels invited us over, and I was so sad that we'd just filled our bellies with breakfast burritos.

They prevailed upon us to take at least something, so we stopped, chatted, and walked away with several donuts apiece and our pockets stuffed with cookies.

I told myself that next summer, I was going to pick a trailhead and be an angel too.

As we began a twelve-mile up-and-down slope that would take us above tree line, A.J. talked constantly about birds and other wildlife. Turned out he was a more-than-amateur bird watcher, and he knew the names of *everything*. Dash had always been crazy for animals, and with A.J., Dash found someone who could really talk about the subject. He listened intently and asked a bunch of questions.

During the second week of our CT journey, Dash and I had noticed a type of bird that seemed quite unafraid of people. They were gray and white with expressive faces. Several of these birds had come really close, either hopping after us on the trail or sitting on nearby branches, cocking their heads and watching us as we passed within a few feet. We'd become rather fond of these birds, but not being a wildlife expert, I had no idea what they were. We'd called them Watcher Birds.

We mentioned this to A.J. and he immediately identified them.

"Oh, those are Camp Robber Jays," he said. "Yeah, they're pretty brave. They'll also steal your food if they get the chance."

"And I thought they just liked us."

"They like your food." A.J. laughed.

A.J. would often stop, pick up a bug and hold it, turn it around in his palm and take pictures of it. Or he'd catch a movement, then stop and level his high-powered camera to snap a picture of a far-off hawk. A.J. named off dozens of birds, bugs, and other creatures. A librarian in Austin, Texas, he was built for research and was an unending fountain of knowledge for Dash.

Eventually, Dash ranged out ahead of us, as had become his habit, and A.J. and I got to reminisce some more about the old days. We laughed and talked about the halls of Durango High School, how he'd run with the theater crowd while I'd run with the Dungeons and Dragons geeks, and we just enjoyed the sunshine, the exercise, and the beautiful vistas.

Though he must have hiked with us for hours, it seemed far too soon when he finally said, "Sorry guys, I'd love to keep going with you, but I gotta get back."

We stopped at a Colorado Trail signpost on the high

tundra, just above the tree line, and he took a picture of Dash and me next to the sign. With friendly waves all around, A.J. turned and began his journey back toward Lake City.

Dash and I turned our faces westward.

We'd heard tell from other hikers that the last week and a half of the trail was the hardest, with high-mountain climbs, thin air, and lots of ups-and-downs. We were in the heart of the Rockies now. Towering peaks surrounded us in every direction.

But what concerned Dash and me the most was that we were headed above tree line and we weren't coming down for forty miles—that's nearly three full segments. It was nothing but high tundra from here all the way to Molas Pass. Morning, evening, and during the deadly noon-to-three window, we'd be exposed.

Just like with Searle Pass, if the lightning came, we'd have nowhere to run.

24

HIGH COUNTRY

THAT HIGH MOUNTAIN TUNDRA took some getting used to. Even with clear skies above, it made me uneasy. It was just...odd. Like something was missing, and I didn't know what it was. I felt like I was living one of my high school stress nightmares. Like I was strolling down the halls, saying hello to friends, then suddenly realized I was wearing no pants!

We were in the wild, but there wasn't a tree in sight. We were high up in the mountains, but the ground was flat. Whenever I thought of the wilderness, I thought of trees. Whenever we'd gone above tree line before, it was always at a sharp upward angle. It created an odd, alien feel to this sun-drenched terrain.

My mind kept searching for the familiar—a stand of aspens in the distance, the beginning of a pine forest—but nothing but rocky outcroppings, tufts of hardy mountain grass, and blue blue sky stretched out before us.

Even the bushes were different. Every now and then we'd hit an enormous patch of rugged, tough-as-nails bushes that went on for half a mile. Those who'd cut the trail had worked hard to make it through this. Those tough little branches were inflexible and as hard as plastic. They grabbed at our packs and legs as we pushed through.

In addition to the alien terrain, "what ifs" abounded in my mind.

What if a thunderstorm moved in? Where would we find shelter?

What if we had to pitch our tent out in the open like this, and high winds blew it away?

What if a bear comes along up here? Where do we put the bear bag?

But as we continued on, the sun stayed high and bright. Fluffy cumulus clouds hung in the sky like ornaments. The wind was mild, and we saw no bears.

We hit the highest point on the entire Colorado Trail that day. The trail makers had posted a sign at the spot. It read:

HIGH POINT
13,271 FT
THE COLORADO TRAIL

A group of college kids lounged by the signpost like lizards in the sun. There were six of them, five young men and one young woman. The dudes were sprawled out, leaning back on their packs like they were in chaise lounges. The lone girl among them crouched by her pack, rummaging through it, looking for something. A couple of the boys had their shirts off, sunbathing. The whole scene made me grin, so I started up a conversation with them.

Their trail names were colorful: Doc, Sunburn, TL, Gordito, Specs, and G Boy. Specs, as you might guess, was sporting some sweet sunglasses. Sunburn, well…it was pretty obvious. Gordito, while his name means "little fat one," was anything but fat. He was one of the boys with his shirt off, and he was ripped enough to belong on the cover of Muscle & Fitness magazine. He also, apparently, spoke fluent Spanish. I didn't get the story behind G Boy's name, and something told me I shouldn't ask. TL stood for Team Leader, and he was the serious one of the group. He sat quietly at the back with his wide-brimmed hat shading his eyes while they goofed around. It was like he'd made it his job to look after these on-the-trail otters, and they deferred to him. Doc was the girl, and she got her name because she was studying pre-med and had the skills—and supplies—to fix up blisters and cuts and such.

We talked for a while, and they were such a delightful group that it gave me hope for the future. They were respectful toward me and they engaged Dash when he stepped up to talk.

Apparently they were just going to hike a portion of the trail together as a group endeavor. They'd started at Segment 22 and planned to hike through to Durango.

They asked what I did and I told them I was a writer. They thought that was cool and asked to hear more, so I gave them the hook for *Summer of the Fetch* and passed out business cards—which I keep handy whether in downtown New York or at the height of the Colorado Trail.

During our conversation, Gordito made a comment about chess.

"Do you play?" I asked them.

"Yeah, but TL's the master," Gordito said. "He's been kicking everybody's butt."

"Oh! You have a chess board with you?" I asked.

"A little one. Magnetic pieces."

"Sweet," I said. "Well, if we all end up camping in the same place tonight, maybe we could play a game."

Several of them whooped. "Absolutely."

TL, as usual, watched coolly from the back of the group.

After a few more minutes of cheerful chatter, Dash and I bid them farewell and headed out.

That afternoon, as we hiked down one of the steeper slopes we'd seen in this high country, we discovered an old mine. The dilapidated log cabin had fallen in upon itself, and Dash explored a really deep hole in the ground nearby. There were also pieces of rusted iron equipment, perhaps some kind of smelting unit?

After we'd taken enough pictures, we continued down the hill, turned a corner, and beheld the most beautiful valley I've ever seen. Majestic peaks rose on either side, and the blue sky rippled with clouds above. Afternoon light speared down, lighting up a dozen shades of breathtaking green. The blue ribbon of the river glimmered, twisting through the bottom of the valley.

"Wow..." I breathed.

"This is my favorite place," Dash said reverently. "We gotta bring Mom here. Can I grab your phone and take pictures?"

"Do it up." I handed him the phone.

He ran ahead, looking for the best vantage points.

We descended halfway down the valley and, that night, we actually did end up staying close to the College Six, as I'd come to call them. They found a fantastic campsite that had a chunk of rock in the middle shaped like a table. It was perfectly flat and just the right height. I considered challenging them to a game of chess that night, but between the early evening clouds and the high ridges, it was almost dark by the time we set up our tent, so I let it go. Dash and I decided to just eat dinner and tuck into our sleeping bags.

The next day dawned bright and sunny, and the valley was just as gorgeous in the morning light as it had been in the evening. With all its grandeur, though, it was what I'd call a "pass-through" valley. In short, there wasn't much to do except gaze at it. Everything was on a slope. The only flat space seemed to be the riverbed far below. Our campsite had been one of the best in the vicinity, and we'd still slept on a slant.

After an oatmeal breakfast, we got onto the trail, hiking up and out of the valley, and I began to think about oatmeal, about how, after three and a half weeks, it was still satisfying. I mean, I have a high tolerance for repetition, but even I get sick of things after a while. Yet I still looked forward to oatmeal for breakfast every morning.

It got me to thinking about scarcity, and about how maybe

it isn't a bad thing. It might, in fact, be a good thing.

At home, I ate whatever I wanted whenever I wanted, and usually of whatever variety I wanted. Cheeseburgers. Cokes. Pasta. Salads with blue cheese. Fried chicken. Lasagna. Food of a hundred different stripes based in a dozen different cultures.

Out here, I ate Clif Bars, oatmeal, dehydrated veggie dinners, beef jerky, tuna packs, and nuts. And I drank water. And that was it. That was the entire variety of my diet. And I ate only enough—barely enough—to fuel my body.

I mean, I wasn't starving all the time. I wasn't so hungry that my energy level plummeted. After all, I'd hike all day and was honestly more energized than I could remember being in the last decade.

No, it was that I ate only what I absolutely needed. Scarcity not only made me energized and happy, but grateful for what I did have.

What if the key to happiness wasn't indulging every desire, but creating a sustainable contrast of scarcity and fulfillment?

It seemed like a crazy notion, coming from a consumer culture where, if you have a more expensive car/house/entertainment system, you're doing "better" than your neighbor. But I'd found a ridiculous amount of happiness on the trail, and there were no luxuries out here. No echelons of more-valuable and less-valuable. The majesty was free to all.

I remembered Bree's declaration when she stood waist-deep in the Cochetopa River. "We don't own the wilderness. Camp wherever you want!"

It made me think about monks, about how they'd deny themselves the trappings of luxury to clear their minds and eliminate the clutter to better hear the voice of their hearts. Scarcity for clarity.

The surreal, tree-less high mountain tundra kept going, rolling greens mixed with rocky outcroppings, and it began to seem more normal to me. And better yet, the skies hadn't threatened us. I found my unease slowly fading.

Unlike some other parts of the trail, there was absolutely nobody up here except thru-hikers and mountain bikers. It was…quiet all around. Inside and outside of my head.

Dash and I spent the day watching pikas as we ate up the miles. Those little rodents were everywhere. They'd pop up in front of us, race away, and dive between the cracks of the tumbledown stones. Then they'd pop back up to perch on the crest of a rock and chatter at us.

We also saw quite a few marmots. They didn't chatter like the pikas. In fact, I don't remember ever hearing a marmot make any sound at all. And they were pretty chill, no bolting about like the pikas—except when there was lightning, of course.

At lunch, we chomped away on our bars and beef jerky and watched a marmot for about half an hour. It perched on top of a rock, staring at us from about a dozen feet away, chewing on the air for so long that Dash began to talk for the marmot like a ventriloquist. Later that day, one marmot let me get about six feet away from it before vanishing into its burrow.

That night, we found a pristine high mountain pond with a wealth of flat spots to camp. As we set up on a flat promontory overlooking the pond, the College Six rolled in and set up on the opposite shore about three hundred feet away. Another hiker named Whirlwind also joined us, and soon we had a bit of an event going on. The Six spent the early afternoon playing in the water. A trio attempted to walk across the entire shallow lake. It was fun to watch them realize just how deep the mud was when they were halfway in. They sank up to their knees and had a fun time washing their legs off afterward.

That afternoon, I walked down to their campground. I found Gordito working on G Boy, massaging out stiff muscles—apparently Gordito was a licensed massage therapist. Doc tended to Specs's blisters. I chatted with them for a while, then challenged anyone who was interested to a chess game. There was a resounding "yes" and we agreed to get together after dinner.

Later that night, as Dash and I ate with Whirlwind, two of

The Six sat on the far shore of the lake and played music. One strummed a small guitar, and the other sang. The music rolled across the lake, creating an unforgettable moment. I just smiled, ate yummy food, and listened.

After dinner, Sunburn came over with the magnetic chess board.

"Excellent." I clapped my hands together, and we fell to playing.

My education in chess came primarily from the two years I'd spent in New York City. I had no formal training. I'd never been part of the chess club in high school, and I'd never been in a tournament of any kind. My father had played chess when I was a kid, and my brother and I used to horse around with the pieces when he wasn't around, but we'd rarely played a full game.

Later in New York, in my early thirties, I worked the graveyard shift at Morgan Stanley in Times Square. That's when I met Denny, a New York native and lifer at Morgan Stanley who referred to chess only as "The Game."

He showed me an alternate world in New York, where the most seemingly-random people knew how to play chess. He and I locked horns on It'sYourMove.com during the lazier moments of our night shift. But beyond the tower of Morgan Stanley and my battles with Denny, I began to notice chess boards everywhere in the city. One night, around two in the morning, I stepped into a convenience store and noticed a board behind the counter. I asked the Pakistani clerk if he played, and he perked up.

"I do," he said. "You?"

"I do," I said.

"Game?" he asked, and that was about all we said to one another. He put the board on the counter—there wasn't another soul in the store—and we played right then and there. I had hope for about five minutes—roughly ten moves in—and then he proceeded to kick my ass. The game lasted a total of fifteen minutes.

Chuckling at how freakin' good he was, I thanked him for

the game and headed out.

I left the convenience store smiling. In New York, you just never knew what you were going to find.

I continued playing night-by-night with Denny, and he told me to do some studying. He recommended I do some reading, too: Bobby Fischer Teaches Chess.

"It's the only book you need," Denny had said. "He says chess is all about going after the king. If you're not actively going after the king, you're just losing slowly."

I read the book cover-to-cover, and it shaped how I approach the game.

I capped off my chess education with a grueling game against Denny a few nights before I left New York City for good. He'd beaten me every single time we'd played before, but in our last game, I got scrappy. He lost focus just long enough for me to stage a comeback. I had only four pieces left to his seven, but I'd been unexpectedly aggressive, unorthodox, and I pinned him against the back row and ended the game. I came away with a win.

It had been my best game ever.

As Sunburn and I set up the board, I enjoyed the anticipation of facing off against someone completely unknown.

"So no TL?" I asked.

"He sent me to test you out first," Sunburn said. "I'm the worst player of the group. If you beat me, he'll send the next up the hill."

Doc had come to watch, and while we played, she wandered around, plucking wildflowers. She gave one to Dash, one to Sunburn, and one to me. It was super cute.

Turns out Sunburn actually didn't know very much about chess. I had to refresh his memory about how a knight moved, and he'd never seen anyone castle before, so I explained that as well. He soaked it up like a sponge.

The game didn't last long. I took his queen after a few moves, then moved in and mated his king.

"Well," he said, sitting back. "Guess I'd better get the next guy."

"Thanks for the game," I said. He grinned and headed down the hill.

TL came up next.

"Oh! Did I skip ahead in the line?" I asked.

TL didn't reply, just smiled and sat down. I was having a good time, and I honestly didn't care whether I won or lost at this point. How many people listened to live music, played chess and ate dinner next to a mountain lake at thirteen thousand feet? This evening was already a win. In fact, it was possible that no one had ever played chess in this spot before today. This was unique. If TL wiped the floor with me, I'd still be grinning.

The sun dipped in the sky, and the temperature dropped. We went from summer heat to autumn brisk in about thirty minutes. I soon began to shiver, but...

I played the best chess of my life.

I remembered Denny's words from New York, and I burst out of the gate going after TL's king with a vengeance. If he was as good as his friends had indicated, I knew I had to put him on his heels right away.

TL stayed cool, meticulously set up his opening. I took early chances.

And I'll be damned if I didn't actually get away with those risks. To my surprise, I pinned his king, queen, and most of his pieces against the back row before he got set up.

He was good. He had hopped his knight across the board just as I'd castled, and in one more move, he would have forked my king and my rook, then he would have proceeded to pick apart my back field. I could see it all just two moves away.

But I never gave him the chance. I checked his king. He blocked. I checked his king again and controlled the pace. He was forced to defend rather than complete his attack.

Check. Check. Check... Check mate.

In a dozen moves, it was over. We'd only captured about five pieces between us.

I wasn't sure what kind of reaction I'd get from him; I was

still stunned at how quickly that had played out. As I said, it was the best game of my life.

He looked surprised, but he was a true gentleman about it.

He reached across the board, and I shook his hand. "Good game," he said genuinely.

Dash had already retired to the tent to trap the warmth, but I wanted to make sure TL had a fair chance at a rematch.

"Again?" I offered.

He just smiled. "No, I'm good. It's getting cold." I was into my third layer already, while TL was still in shorts and a T-shirt. I didn't understand why he wasn't absolutely blue with cold. Ah, youth.

"Great game. That fork would have killed me."

"If only I'd gotten there," he said. "Thanks for playing."

"Maybe if we end up at the same campsite down the road, we can have that rematch," I said.

"You got it."

TL headed back down the hill, and that was the last I would see of the College Six. I wasted no time clambering into the tent with Dash.

"Brrrr. Cold out there," I said, but the tent was already toasty warm. "Hey, did you see? Your old man didn't do too badly."

Dash had his winter hat on and was snuggled down into his bag. All I could see were his eyes and his nose. "Are you bragging?" He hated bragging.

I laughed. "I suppose I am. I'll stop. Good night, buddy. Love you."

"Love you, too." He rolled over, and we both went to sleep.

25

THE WATERFALL

THE NEXT MORNING, we passed into Segment 24, which Dash would later describe as his absolute favorite of the entire trail. The high country continued for another nine miles before opening up to the most beautiful vista yet. We stood at nearly thirteen thousand feet looking down at a gorge that cut deep through the mountains. On the left side of the gorge, a jagged ridge shot into the sky. Straight ahead, miles in the distance, purple and red mountains formed a background that looked painted. To the right, lower than the ridge, lay a high mountain lake on a flat plateau. The lake went almost to the edge of the cliff.

We just stood there, stunned.

"It doesn't even look real," I murmured.

"This is the most beautiful thing I've ever seen," Dash said for the fourth—and what would turn out to be the final—time.

I suppose there's only so long a person can stand in awestruck gratitude, so we eventually moved along.

I pulled out the Data Book to check the lay of the land. The elevation was about to drop four thousand feet over the next nine miles, half of it in the first *two* miles.

In short, that's damned steep, but numbers don't do it justice. We stood on the edge of the precipice, and that slope just went down and down.

Dash must have seen my reluctance at so much downhill, so he smiled at me. "Hey, we get back into the trees today."

I laughed and we started down. As we navigated the back-and-forth of the switchbacks, I let my mind wander. Tomorrow we'd reach Molas Pass, our last supply stop before the end, and we would meet up with Nancy and her two daughters, Raeden and Mallory. After that, the final leg of the journey.

Damn. We were almost done!

We'd been hiking for almost four weeks now. My feet were nearly one hundred percent, and Dash and I could hike all day, no matter the elevation gain or the thinning air. It had all become routine.

I let myself drift into the future, to the moment where I'd sit in a chair with a drink in my hand, put my feet up, and look back on this with satisfaction…and I forgot the first, most important rule. Remember my list of the seven things I needed to focus on? Yeah. I lost focus on one of the six that could kill me.

And I almost died for it.

Switchbacks are designed to be gradual. They're made to turn steep ground into a longer, gentler descent. But the trail was still on the side of mountain, a damned steep one. Step off the path, and it's almost straight down. The path was dusty and gravely, especially at the turnarounds of each switchback, where loose bits of rocks collected.

As I was turning right at a switchback, I put my left foot onto one of those patches of gravel without thinking.

I slipped, and my heel skidded off the edge.

With a grunt, I twisted my leg at the last instant, pivoting my weight from heel to ball-of-foot and catching the edge of the trail before I went over. I'd racked up hours of training at the Family Taekwondo Center of Littleton, practicing that exact pivot for spinning hook kicks. My body just did it instinctively.

It all happened in a fraction of a second. Twitch twitch!

A tumble of rocks cascaded down. If I'd been even an inch further west, I'd have gone over.

My martial arts training had just saved my life.

But it came at a price. Something went 'clunk' in my knee, followed by a sharp stab of pain. I hastily scrambled away from the edge with a hiss. Unlike the intentional pivot of a spinning hook kick—where I instigated the twist, stayed on balance, and spun like a weathervane—this stumble had been sudden and unexpected. I'd had to put all my weight on my left leg during the twist to catch that ledge.

"Dad!" Dash cried out. He'd seen me stumble, and he ran back up the trail toward me. He looked spooked, and I think he realized what had almost happened. If I had gone over, he wouldn't have been able to do anything except watch me tumble down.

"I, um, slipped," I said lightly, testing my knee.

"You okay?"

"I'm fine," I said, but I wasn't at all sure. After that first burst of pain, my knee had stopped hurting. I tested it again, and it held my weight. It didn't feel like I'd torn anything, but that 'clunk' had scared me. What if I'd torn something and I just didn't feel it yet?

I tentatively started down the trail, taking it easy on my knee and staying the hell away from the edge.

Everything seemed to be fine.

When we reached the bottom of the switchbacks, there was a mine shaft dug straight into the mountainside, a perfect rectangular doorway. It also happened to be at our four-hundred-mile mark. Dash and I took pictures outside the mine, then dared the interior.

There is nothing like the sensation of being in a cave.

I'd gone spelunking once in Tennessee, in deep caves with bends and tunnels that wound far away from the tiny opening, so far that one experiences absolute darkness. It's far different than darkness in one's house, or on a moonless, starless night. Absolute darkness is terrifying. It had been my one and only spelunking adventure, and it wasn't for me. I'd felt trapped and constantly disoriented. Add the absolute darkness and…nope. Hang me off a cliff. Speed me down the highway in a car. Drop me out of an airplane. I'm good. But don't stick me under the earth.

However, this mine shaft wasn't like those Tennessee caves. This was made by people, arrow straight, and it only went into the mountain about fifty feet. That, I could handle. Besides, I had a flashlight and a backup flashlight. And I never lost sight of that rectangular doorway of sunlight. So Dash and I had fun goofing around and taking pictures.

After that, we hiked further down the slope—which was less pronounced now—and found a ruined mining shack. We horsed around there for about fifteen minutes, then continued on, following the creek lower and lower.

Elk Creek was fascinating. We saw copper-colored rocks, places where thick, spongy, day-glow green moss lined the river, and we found a crystal clear pool. It looked like something orchestrated, like a hot tub crafted by a five-star Hyatt Resort. Yet here it was, free for anyone who hiked the trail.

But, of course, it was no hot tub. That water was maybe two degrees above freezing.

I paused, took some pictures of the pool. I even entertained the idea of stripping down to my boxers and testing it out….

But I didn't.

I wistfully said goodbye and we soldiered on.

The trail angled north and hitched up against the side of an intimidating red cliff wall. It actually leaned over us. The thing was easily a thousand feet tall, and it gave the uneasy impression that it was about to fall over.

Along the base of that leaning red wall ran a series of rock stair steps that were either naturally occurring or had been carved out of the rock. It seemed unlikely that they would have just formed like that, but it seemed almost as unlikely that someone would have carved them. I could only imagine what kind of equipment, time, and energy that would have taken. However it had happened, the rough staircase seemed like it had been made for giants. Each step was about two feet tall.

By this time, I had forgotten all about my left knee. I'd chalked it up to just a minor tweak that had already faded. But after a dozen heavy steps down, the knee gave. It felt like someone had stabbed a dagger underneath my kneecap. I stumbled into the cliff wall, hissing.

"Dad?" Dash immediately came back to check on me.

We stopped, and I rested. The pain faded pretty quickly, so I dared the steps again, feeling a vague foreboding. Sure enough, after another three steps, I got that "dagger under the kneecap" again and had to stop. Dash, oblivious this time, kept hopping down the trail.

There had to be a hundred steps here. If I couldn't go more than three without that unbelievable pain, I wasn't going to make it to the bottom, let alone to the end of the segment.

"Got a problem here, Dash," I said. He spun around and, like a billy goat, bounded back to me.

"Knee?" he asked.

"I'm going to have to try something different." I tried not to think of what it meant if my 'something different' didn't work. I envisioned a stretcher. Dash would have to hike on alone while I waited for him to bring help.

I stood up again. No pain. And there hadn't been any going down the gradual slope. Only when I bent the knee did it buckle.

So...no bending the knee.

Rather than "step left, step right, step left, step right" down the stairs, I did what little kids do when stairs are too big. I led with my hurt leg, keeping it straight while bending my right leg to take the weight. Lead with the left, bend the right, lead with the left, bend the right. My right leg didn't like that. It got seriously fatigued after about a dozen steps, but it held.

And I avoided those stabs of pain.

Once we got on more-or-less even ground again, I tested my left leg and it seemed to be fine, but I vowed I wasn't going to push it. From here to Molas Pass was only about three more miles of gradual downhill, then four more miles of uphill. Uphills were not the problem, so I just had to make those three miles.

We reached the tree line again, and I breathed a sigh of relief for a different reason. I had actually come to love that exposed country high above the trees, but a part of me had always been holding my breath, waiting for the lightning to come.

Down here, if a storm came, we could just keep walking and talking, letting the rain slide off our slickers without fear of being impaled by a crackling, three-hundred-million-volt electrical death spear. Down here, the air was thicker, warmer. The boughs of the trees cut the constant sun, and the sounds of woodland animals—birds, squirrels, ptarmigans—returned in a comforting, background cadence.

I felt like I had come home. We were safely back in the arms of the woods...

...which was when we ran into the aftermath of an avalanche that had obliterated the trail.

Apparently there had been an unusually high number of powerful avalanches in Colorado in 2018. Dash and I had seen evidence of a couple of these back at the beginning of the second week, but they had all been well away from the trail, cast down far below, nothing more than a view-appreciation-moment.

This one had completely obliterated the trail. Our progress was blocked by a thousand tall pine trees ripped from their moorings and cast down the slope like toothpicks. They'd fallen every which way, sticking up at every angle. The devastation continued hundreds of feet up the slope to our right, all the way down to the river to our left, and even up the slope on the far side beyond the river.

Dash and I stopped, gaping, awed by the sheer power it had taken to treat hundred-foot-tall trees like this. Every one of them weighed as much as a car—about two tons—which meant, if one happened to roll over on us while we were clambering over it, it'd crush us.

There was no way to go around. We'd have to climb up spiny log after spiny log until we reached the other side where the trail emerged.

"Nothing for it," I said.

"We're log hopping," Dash replied. He went first, ducking under high trunks, jumping onto the lower trunks. Sometimes he'd walk along a tree that angled higher and higher, then jump down to another below it. At first as I watched him, I worried. One bad tumble could cause a significant injury. But he was so confident and sure-footed that I soon put it from my mind. Time to focus. Time to make sure Dash didn't have to look after his old dad because I didn't pay attention to my own footing.

I gamely followed.

After stepping on a couple of the logs, my fears about one rolling over on me diminished. The weight that had jammed these logs together had been far heavier than I was. Even if I jumped up and down on one, I didn't think it would budge.

Still…it wasn't like this haphazard pile had been designed by an engineer. Who knew which of these trees was a lever that would unlock the jam and send everything tumbling down the slope?

I chose my steps with care.

Which presented the next challenge. Even assuming the logs didn't shift and fall on me, there was no guarantee I wouldn't fall on them, or between them. Hopping from trunk to trunk without making a misstep wasn't easy. I wobbled, caught my balance, stepped to the next trunk. No wobble. Stepped to the next trunk. Lost my balance. Grabbed out for a branch. Caught it. It bowed and, luckily, didn't break, and I regained my balance.

I looked below. It was about a six-foot drop to a latticework of smaller logs and branches, some of them sticking straight up. The entire landslide was bristling with stakes. One bad fall and I could impale myself. Or break an ankle.

Try walking an uneven—and possibly unstable—balance beam with a pit of spikes all around you while balancing a fifty-pound pack. That'll give you an idea of what it was like.

I hopped to another log. Another hop. Another grab for a branch to steady myself. Over and over and over again. I paid special attention to my left knee, but it didn't let me down.

We made it to the other side with only one injury. Dash had actually grabbed a branch that broke off. When he'd flailed to catch himself he had fallen and cut his hand on one of those aforementioned spikes. It left a pretty good cut, but we bandaged it up and he seemed fine.

"Okay, that was a pain in the ass," I said, once we were through. "But also kind of fun."

"I cut my hand," he said.

"Yeah, but before that. Like American Gladiators."

"I cut my hand!" he restated, but he was smiling.

"At least we're past it," I said.

Right?

Wrong.

It turned out that avalanche was only one of four between us and our intended campsite. We had to traverse each one of them in the same fashion, and they got progressively worse. I kept thinking that my knee was going to buckle as we hopped over those logs, or that I'd make a misstep and have a broken ankle to go with my twitchy knee.

But by the time we got to the fourth one, Dash had become accustomed to navigating them, and he took off ahead of me, hopping deftly log-to-log and then down on the far side by the time I was only halfway.

A moment later, after he'd vanished into the woods, he whistled back to check on me, asking without words if I was okay.

When we got past the fourth and final avalanche tree-fall, we rolled into a long stretch of level ground with beautiful spots perfect for camping, a confluence of Elk Creek and another small tributary.

"I like this," I said. "Let's take a break and filter some water." We plopped our packs down and pulled out the Platypus.

Though we had miles yet to go to reach our mileage goal, I wasn't in a hurry. Every moment I let my knee rest was a good moment.

We did a little exploring. Dash went to check out a spot we'd seen on Elk Creek where the water had looked milky white because of the chalk-colored rocks beneath the surface. I wandered upstream along the tributary, following a barely-visible side trail that diverged from the CT. I rounded the edge of a cliff face...

...and it opened up to reveal a tall, misty waterfall.

"Holy crap," I murmured. Yes, I actually said "holy crap" to no one.

I loved these little surprises hidden around the most unlikely corners on the Colorado Trail. With a grin, I headed down the trail to tell Dash.

He, of course, raced back to the waterfall and loved it even more than I had—though he didn't proclaim it as his new favorite spot. That was still reserved for that final overlook of Segment 24.

While he was exploring that path, I returned to my pack, got the Platypus, and plunked down to finish filtering the water. As I did, who should appear through the woods but Jack!

Dash and I had thought he'd left us behind at Segment 18, but apparently he'd taken a Zero Day or two since we'd crossed paths, and he'd just now caught up to us. Dash returned from the waterfall and was delighted. The two of them shot the breeze like old buddies.

As they did, another hiker we didn't know stopped and joined the conversation. The new hiker's name was Tony, and he and Jack knew each other from earlier on the trail. By the time we'd all gotten acquainted, Bree showed up!

It was like a reunion of old friends. We'd only met Bree

once before, and Jack twice, but it felt more profound than that. Perhaps the social deprivation of the trail made encountering even one familiar face a cause for celebration. Or maybe all Colorado Trail hikers simply have a higher chance to make a deep connection because of our love of the wilderness.

We chatted and the afternoon wore on. The charm of the woods, the river, the waterfall, and the unexpected company was so wonderful, I decided racking up another few miles today simply wasn't important. So at two-thirty, I suggested to Dash that we just camp here.

He agreed.

It was the earliest we'd ever stopped hiking, and the shortest distance we'd ever hiked in a day—only seven miles—but it felt right. I'd rest my knee, we'd enjoy the heat of the afternoon, and I could grab my first high mountain bath in the pool beneath the glorious waterfall.

We tried to talk Jack and Bree into staying the night as well, to make a party of it. But both had made promises to meet other people farther down the trail. So after about an hour, we reluctantly said goodbye. That actually *was* the last time we saw them both, but it was a quality send-off. It just doesn't get better than that.

And we'd made a new friend in Tony, who agreed that this *was* quite the spot and decided to make camp with us. We shared dinner and stories. Tony told us about hanging bear bags in Yosemite when he was nineteen years old. They'd used the recommended guidelines—ten feet up and six feet away from the trunk—but they'd run into a relentless, acrobatic bear. Tony and his friends had watched it climb the trunk, shimmy out onto the limb, and they'd watched the limb bend almost to the ground. But the bear hadn't let go, just kept swiping at the saddle-bagged sacks until he fell. Then he'd rolled to his feet, climbed the tree, and tried again. He'd tried again, fallen again.

Undeterred, the bear had finally snagged one of the bags as he fell, bringing it with him. Once he'd hit the ground, he'd ripped the bag apart and devoured everything inside.

Tony said they'd managed to save the second bag, and when they'd cowboy-camped the next night, he'd awoken the following morning with the bear standing over him, its face less than a foot way, so close he could feel its breath on his cheek.

He said he hadn't freaked out, had just waited, frozen, as the bear sniffed him. Then the bear had moved on without hurting anyone.

Needless to say, Tony didn't swear by the bear-bag hanging method.

"A determined bear will get the food anyway," he said. "Nothing you can do."

We finished the night with full bellies and the warm feeling of camaraderie, and with hearty goodnights, we all turned in.

26

A DANGEROUS SHOWER

THE NEXT DAY marked the beginning of our final week. As morning dawned on August 11th, we'd officially been on the trail for four full weeks. We'd made our big mistakes and learned from them. Our rhythm matched the rhythm of the trail. And nature felt like home.

During a short stretch where I could get cell reception, I called Nancy. Her home, where we would relax when we'd finished the trail, had transformed into a utopian paradise in our minds. I told her where we were, and we firmed up the final plans: Nancy's oldest daughter Mallory would meet us at Molas Lake and bring our final supply drop. Then Nancy herself would meet us a mile farther up the trail at Little Molas Lake. She'd bring her youngest daughter, Raeden, who was going to hike with us for the final leg of the journey.

We reached Molas Lake early that afternoon. The quaint little mountain destination had boat rentals, a little cabin convenience store, and a half-dozen pay-showers. It was a blessed slice of civilization that, in lieu of a full Zero Day, we planned to use to the fullest.

Not long after, Mallory rolled up in her red SUV like some mythical goddess of the harvest. Not only did she bring us our supplies for the next week—plenty of hiking food and fresh clothes—but she brought a picnic that could have fed half a dozen people, including blueberries, apples, soda, two kinds of potato chips, and a Tupperware full of turkey sandwiches with mayo, lettuce, and ripe tomatoes. We tucked in with gusto and finished just about everything.

After we'd happily distended our bellies, Mallory presented us with two tall thermoses of hot water.

"For the showers," Mallory said. "Just in case."

This is a hat tip to Nancy. I'm in awe of people who can plan for all the contingencies. Nancy is one of those. Not in a million years would I have thought of something so clever. Extra hot water for the showers! I hadn't even known there were showers up here until we arrived!

"Your mom is amazing," I said. I took the thermos, my towel, and a change of fresh clothes from the box Mallory had brought, and headed off for the showers.

When I first saw that a shower token was five dollars, I thought, *Hey, what a bargain. Five dollars for a shower? That's well worth it.*

I breezed right by the part that said the token is only good for two minutes, and just how little shower time that was. Two minutes? Five minutes? Ten minutes? How long does a good shower take? I mean, who times themselves?

I was about to discover: two minutes is *nothing*!

I spent the first minute just trying to get the water temperature adjusted. The shower clicked off before I'd even finished sudsing up my hair. I realized in a flash that this was how the convenience store made its money. Taking a normal-length shower was going to cost thirty dollars!

Good thing Nancy had thought ahead. I would need that water she'd sent. And it was a good thing I'd bought a token for Dash and had it with me. Eyes stinging, I fumbled for Dash's token.

But as I picked it up and poised it over the slot—one eye

blinking and one eye shut—I stopped.

The next two minutes weren't going to go any slower than the first two, and if I didn't want to stalk across the parking lot to buy more tokens, towel wrapped around me with sudsy water dripping down my head, I was going to have to get smart. Time to use Nancy's gift.

Wiping awkwardly at my eyes with the inside of my elbow, I reached around the stall to get the thermos. I uncapped it, raised it, and almost poured it on my sudsy head.

My intuition tapped on the back of my neck.

I heard Mallory's voice. *This is hot water for your shower.*

She'd said hot water. She hadn't said *how* hot.

I'd imagined it to be shower-temperature hot. Why? Because that's what I wanted it to be. I had banished any further contemplation of it.

But if four weeks in the wilderness had taught me anything, it was that just because I *wanted* something to be a certain way didn't mean it was. In fact it rarely meant that.

I brought the thermos down and poured some over my finger.

"Jesus!" I yelped and nearly dropped the thermos. That had come straight out of a tea kettle! It was hot enough to make soup!

My finger prickled, burned from its momentary contact with the water, and my heart pounded at the thought that I'd almost poured that thing over my head. I'd almost done it. That would have been a trip to the hospital for sure.

Who knew taking a shower could suddenly get so dangerous?

Now the suds in my eyes didn't seem so bad. I stepped back out of the stall, dumped half the steaming water down the sink and filled it back up with cold water—the sink water didn't cost a token—until it was the perfect temp.

Before using my last token, I soaped up completely and used the no-longer-deadly thermos water to wash most of it away. Then I used the final token and enjoyed a minuscule two minutes of real shower.

I left the shower cabin refreshed, bought a couple more tokens for Dash, and headed back to the picnic table.

"Well, that was an ordeal," I said.

Dash perked up. A new adventure?

"Beware the thermos." I tapped Dash's full thermos. "It's boiling hot. Pour that on your skin and you'll be sorry."

"How do I use it?" he asked.

"Dump out half, fill the rest with cold water."

"Ah."

"And the shower's going to go quicker than you think." I dropped two tokens into his hands. "Use it strategically."

"Everything on the trail has a trick to it," Dash said.

"Hey! That's exactly what I was thinking."

Without another word, Dash headed off to the showers.

Mallory and I got a chance to catch up. It was really great seeing her. I'd known her since she was a toddler, and now she was in her mid-twenties. She'd finished high school, college, and had been out on her own for a couple of years. But I still thought of her as that quiet, serious little girl who watched me from a distance whenever the extended family got together.

I tend to be boisterous in groups, always telling stories or making dramatic gestures, quick to play a board game or take a trip to the park. In the early years, I would take on the long-limbed, sharp-clawed, googly-eyed form of a velociraptor and chase the kids around the yard.

Most children under four years old are scared of me when we meet for the first time. Who is this big loud man who runs around and chases children? They keep a wary distance.

But by the second time, they begin to test me to see if I'm safe. By the third time, they know I'm for real, that I'm ready to be as ridiculous and imaginative as they can stand, and then I become the best toy in the world. They're constantly tugging on my hand to come play Velociraptor or Cake Monster—a variant of the game "tag" where I capture all the children, put them on a bench or a table, then "bake" them into a cake for the "monster" to eat.

So this was really the first adult conversation I'd ever had with Mallory, and it was wonderful. No Velociraptor this time. Time marches on.

Dash came back from the shower, long hair tousled into a ridiculous snarl. I wondered if we were going to have to shave his head when this was all over. I wouldn't want to attempt pulling a comb through that. Ouch.

Dash didn't seem to care. He sat down, picked through some of the leftovers and nibbled on a candy bar we'd gotten at the convenience store. While chatting with Mallory, I'd organized and packed up our belongings. We were ready to rock.

"Well, I'd best get going," Mallory said. Dash and I helped her load up the boxes with our dirty clothes and the small bit of leftover food from the picnic.

"Thank you so much for coming," I said. "This was delightful. It was great talking with you."

"You, too," she said. "You're one of my favorite uncles."

"Awww," I said.

"I mean, you get narrowly beat out by Uncle Sean."

"Sean *is* funnier than I am." Sean, Nancy's brother, was the kind of guy who had no filter. He consistently blurts the most inappropriate comments at exactly the wrong—right?—moments. He is hilarious. I've told him that when we're old men, I plan to find his nursing home and go there, just so I can die laughing.

We hugged Mallory goodbye and she drove off. We had less than a mile to hike to reach Little Molas Lake which, unlike Molas Lake, had campsites.

After playing *Frogger* with the cars on Highway 550, we came down a gentle grade to the beautiful Little Molas Lake. The northwest shore seemed the most popular. There were a number of cars parked there, and a number of tents set up. So, of course, we preferred to plunk down in a quiet piece of the forest on the western shore. Afternoon turned into evening and we relaxed in the tent, playing *Stack* on my phone. Dash beat me every time.

The sun was almost touching the horizon when Nancy,

Raeden, and their charming family friend showed up.

Nancy—bless her generous soul—had brought cheeseburgers, fries, and drinks—Izze Sparkling for Dash and Mike's Hard Lemonade for me. We sat by the lake, stuffed our faces again, and shot the breeze as a beautiful sunset blossomed in the west. It was blissful. Good company. Great family. And ahhhh…cheeseburgers.

After thanking Nancy profusely for being our avatar of support for this last leg of the journey, we said our goodbyes.

We helped Raeden set up her tent, and I hung the bear bags—we now had two. After all the dishes were cleaned and last-minute camp duties squared away, we congregated in Raeden's larger tent. We laughed and joked and talked trail philosophy.

My kids were half a decade younger than Nancy's kids, but at family gatherings, Raeden and Mallory would always descend upon Dash and Elo and take them off on some fun adventure. They'd been like older siblings, acting as though it was their family duty to entertain the little ones. I always appreciated that, and I never forgot it.

Raeden is bright-eyed and athletic with a dry sense of humor. She was a high school soccer star, and I remember watching her kick ass at a competition in Denver. Now she was grown, newly graduated from college. In fact, she'd been all set to go into the Peace Corps before COVID hit and cancelled the trip.

We all fell into a companionable camaraderie instantly. She enjoyed our trail stories and our irreverent jokes—Uncle Sean had built up her tolerance long ago. That first night, we stayed up late, just gabbing and playing silly games.

"Okay, if we're hoping to get fifteen miles tomorrow, we'd better get some sleep," I finally said.

Dash and I wished her a good night and retired to our tent, where we promptly crashed.

27

ORDINARY MAGIC

THE NEXT FEW DAYS went the way I had originally envisioned the entire trip going, back when we were mistily dreaming about hiking the whole Colorado Trail. Good exercise. Fresh air. Beautiful vistas. Unique encounters with nature. In short: pure enjoyment of the outdoors.

We crossed streams. We summited mountains. I took pictures of a weathered, felled tree that looked like a Viking ship, complete with branches thrust out like oars and thick exposed roots curved upward into a dragon's head prow.

We saw a flock of ptarmigans, and Dash named them. My favorite was Magubis the Force Chicken.

We stood stunned before a lake full of tadpoles halfway into their transformation to frogs. They were huge, maybe as long as my hand from wrist to fingertips, and there were hundreds of them darting this way and that.

We crossed the four-hundred-and-fifty-mile mark. Some hiker had written "450" in sticks by the side of the trail.

We saw a vein of chalk-white rock—a wall of it alongside the trail—with an enormous tree perched above it, its roots slithering around the rock like possessive tentacles.

We camped in beautiful spots, one of which was right on the edge of a cliff by a rollicking stream. Just uphill of us, the stream came down a couple of waterfalls, creating rocky pools where filling up the Platypus was easy. If one was so inclined, one could take a bath there, too. I wasn't so inclined this time, but I accidentally glimpsed a young couple doing just that as I first rounded the bend. I averted my gaze and smirked. They vanished and appeared again fully dressed. I'd never seen anyone put on clothes that fast.

On August 13th, we hiked over Blackhawk Pass, our penultimate trip above twelve thousand feet. Raeden, Dash, and I took our "summit-selfies" as the wind blew our hair all about.

Raeden started down first, but Dash lingered for a moment. I almost went ahead of him, but he'd turned to face the way we'd come, so I stopped. He remained silent, and I hiked the few feet back up to stand next to him.

He looked back over the way we'd come: that seemingly never-ending horizon of peaks, the same peaks we'd seen when we'd stood with Gretchen that first night. Except this time, we were on the other side of them.

Dash glanced up at me, then back at the mountains. "We came over all of that," he said, echoing my thoughts. "We started where the ground was flat on the far side, and we came up and over all of it."

"We sure did," I said.

"Kind of hard to believe," he said.

"It is," I agreed.

"I'm so glad," he said. "I'm so glad we did this."

I didn't say anything at first because, you know, it's kind of hard to talk when you have a lump in your throat.

"Well," I finally managed, clapping a hand on his back. "Only one more twelve-thousand-foot peak to get over."

"And it's all downhill from there." He smirked at me.

"Ouch."

On August 14th, I crested the final twelve-thousand-foot

peak, Indian Trail Ridge, alone. I had ranged out ahead of Dash and Raeden for this final climb. She was still adjusting to the high altitude, and her climbing pace was a little slower than ours. So Dash had elected to wait for her just before the ascent while I went on ahead to save us a camping spot at Taylor Lake on the other side. We'd passed several hikers along the trail that day, and every single one of them said they were camping at Taylor Lake tonight. I wanted to make sure we had a good campsite.

Indian Trail Ridge connected two peaks, actually. It looked like something out of a *Lord of the Rings* movie, a place hobbits would have crossed to get to Mordor. It was a natural stone bridge from peak to peak, a few hundred feet apart. Sharp, bare cliffs fell away on either side as I walked across, a thousand foot drop if I strayed too far in either direction—like some crazy fantasy walkway connecting one jagged castle to another.

I tried to stop and enjoy it, to imagine I was Aragorn surveying the battle ahead, but the wind pushed forcefully through that notch. When I lost my balance and was taken by a sudden, terrifying vertigo, I settled for a quick, appreciative glance and hurried through.

Coming down off that ridge didn't lead into the smoldering desolation of Mordor, but rather to the majestic Taylor Lake, a dark blue body of water nestled among light and dark greens far below. From my vantage point, the lake looked tiny and perfect, with a ring of mountains behind it. It was like something from an oil painting, and I paused to appreciate it.

This last bit was the final time I'd be above tree line. After a quiet moment to mark the occasion, I started down the winding switchbacks.

And that's when my imagination went wild.

This was the first time I'd left Dash so far behind that, if he happened to get into trouble, there was no way I'd even hear him, let alone be able to reach him in time. Each time before when I had ranged out ahead, which had mostly been in the first week, we'd never been out of shouting distance for more than a minute.

It began to prey on my mind.

I imagined a mountain lion. Yeah. Not a bear, but a sneaky mountain lion seeing me leave my young behind. I envisioned it creeping up through the brush, starving, tail twitching as it watched Dash lounging on his pack, lost in his thoughts as he waited for Raeden.

Now is the time, the mountain lion would think. *Now is the moment to spring, to tear, to rend and bite.*

I imagined it leaping upon him. I imagined Dash fighting for all he was worth, but caught by surprise, he just couldn't match the lion's ferocity—

I actually stopped on the trail, my heart pounding wildly, thinking I'd just left my son to die. The more I thought of it, the more I couldn't shake the feeling. A cold fear settled over me, the worst I'd had since we ran for our lives on Searle Pass.

What if I'd made a horrible mistake? What if my intuition was warning me, like with the scalding thermos water?

If I'd been a thousand yards away from him, I'd surely have turned back. But Dash was two miles behind me. I swallowed and told myself I was just imagining things. I told myself to focus on my job. To trust him to take care of himself. We'd made a plan. I should stick to it. I didn't turn back for him but continued toward the lake. Still, I descended that long, steady trail cut into the edge of the mountain reluctantly.

I reached the bottom of the mountain and wound my way through the head-high brush to Taylor Lake, found a campsite, and dropped my stuff.

The switchbacks down the mountain were in plain view, towering over the lake, and I watched them intently. I saw hikers coming down like colorful ants in an ant farm. None of them were Dash or Raeden.

After I'd set everything up, I wound my way back through the brush—another natural maze like the one by the Cochetopa River—and went to the base of the trail. Still no Dash or Raeden.

I had just come to the decision to grab a water bottle, the bear spray, and sprint back up the trail when I saw two hikers round the corner at the top of the ridge. They were so tiny I couldn't make out details, but one of them was a bright splash of orange. Dash's backpack was orange. Raeden's was green, and that second figure could definitely be green, though it was harder to tell against the green-and-brown backdrop of the mountainside.

They came closer. It was them. I let out a long sigh of relief. Okay. Not intuition. Just stupid-ass fears.

I waited for them, and as we walked through the maze back to camp, I told Dash about my mountain lion premonition.

He laughed. "A mountain lion? Really?"

"'With nasty big pointy teeth,'" I quoted Monty Python.

"You're kind of dumb, you know?" he said. "But I mean that as a compliment."

"Oh, well then... Wait, how is that a compliment?"

He smiled enigmatically and kept walking.

It turned out we were right about all the CT hikers converging on this final beautiful camping spot. A large group of them clustered together, putting their tents down in a circle just up the hill from us. And they. Threw. A party.

Dash went over to visit them, and they welcomed him with open arms, each giving him a bit of candy they'd saved up.

There were still twenty-two miles left until the end of the trail, but everyone seemed to agree that this was the last night. Dash, Raeden, and I had originally planned to hike fifteen miles tomorrow and save a short seven for our planned last day: August 16th.

But the more we thought about it, the more we considered one last big push.

"Think you could make twenty-two miles?" I asked them both. "Dash, you could have your fried chicken sandwich with pasta Alfredo one day earlier. What do you think?"

"I think I could do it," Raeden said simply.

"I don't know why you're trying to convince me," Dash said. "It's only twenty-two miles. And it's downhill. You're the one who's going to be falling behind."

"Tough talk," I said.

"Bet," he said.

We decided to go out with a bang.

The next morning, we got up early and actually got onto the trail by six-thirty. We were all refreshed and we moved smoothly down the trail at the beginning, though I paid close attention to my knee. The trail went down, down, down. Eleven thousand feet. Ten thousand feet.

The moment we dropped below nine thousand feet, the day became ridiculously hot. I'd underestimated just how much the high altitude had cut the heat and humidity. The dry environs of Durango actually felt downright muggy.

Dash still led, Raeden came after, and as he'd predicted, I lagged behind. The heat and exertion started to take a toll on me. Maybe it was because I could feel the finish line or something. But after twelve miles, the spots of my original blisters—now mostly calluses—started to hurt again. It was a bone-deep hurt, like they needed more than just a night's rest to get back to normal. My ankles had also started to ache, finally feeling the effects of carrying so much weight for so long, I guess. It felt like the cartilage between my foot and leg had flattened, like I was a hair's breadth away from bone hitting bone.

We ran out of food five miles from the end of the trail, and we ran out of water two miles after that. We were in a hurry now, though, and nobody wanted to stop and spend thirty minutes filtering water. Not when we only had three miles to go.

The miracle of cell phone reception returned, and Raeden called Nancy to let her know we were arriving tonight instead of tomorrow. And could she pick us up? Nancy said she was right in the middle of something, but she'd send Robert, Raeden's dad.

And so it was that, about two miles from the end of the

trail, Robert came riding over the hill toward us on his mountain bike. I was parched, starved, and the anticipation of ending the trail had become my singular focus. We'd kept a strong pace the last five days, but this final twenty-two mile push in the heat had really taken it out of me.

Robert is tall and lean, athletic like the rest of the Shanks, and Scottish. He has a light—or heavy if he pours it on—Scottish accent, and when he came around the bend with a day-pack stuffed with food and water, he looked and sounded like a White Knight, the sun at his back, limning him in golden light.

He dismounted, unshouldered his pack, and took out sandwiches, apples, and Reese's Peanut Butter Cups. He'd also brought six liters of water.

We ate everything. We drank everything. I felt rejuvenated again.

Robert left Raeden the keys to a car he'd parked at the trailhead, saying he preferred to bike home. That's right. Home. We were that close.

We started out again as Robert disappeared on his mountain bike. As expected, Raeden and Dash moved faster than I did, ranging out ahead. I ambled along, actually enjoying the solitude. I felt the sense, as I drew nearer the road, that I'd been here before. The curve of the river alongside the trail seemed familiar. The flat rocks beside the water—perfect for sitting with a high school friend and talking juvenile philosophy—seemed like places I'd been before. I had a random flash that I might have kissed a girl somewhere along this stretch, sometime in those teenage years when everything was so vibrant, so exciting, so scary. Back when I had no safety net. I couldn't remember that nameless girl's face. I just had the jolt of something nearly forgotten—or half-imagined—the warmth of her cheek against mine, the press of her lips, the smell of her hair.

Nostalgia overwhelmed me, and I floated along on it, winding through the trees.

I was coming back to the place I'd grown up, coming back

to the place I'd called home once upon a time. Who I'd been, what this place had meant to me, were snapshots on a river that had floated downstream long ago.

I'd been a frightened teenager in this place, exposed to a big scary world, armed only with dreams and the determination of youth.

Now I was fifty. I'd replaced the frightened teenager with a magic hunter long ago. I'd become a Teflon adventurer, accountable to no one. And finally I'd become a father, a man who made commitments and kept them.

The wooded trail finally diverged from the river and opened onto a wide field. A few hundred yards ahead was the end, marked by a sign and a line of knee-high boulders bordering the parking lot. Dash and Raeden jogged back toward me.

"Dad, we didn't cross the line," he said. "We dropped our packs and came back. We should all finish together. Come on, hurry! Here, I'll take your pack for you." He held out his hands.

"No, no, I got it," I said, picking up my pace. "I'm coming. I'm coming."

As we crossed that line of rocks between the field and the parking lot, I felt it for the first time, the magic I'd been searching for my whole life. And the funny thing was…it was everywhere. It was in the adventures of my youth. It was in my marriage to Lara. It was in the lives of my daughter and my son. It was in all my triumphs and failures. It was in every choice I'd made that had led me here.

That magic had brought Dash up short before the end of the trail, had turned him around and made him run back to me so we could finish together.

An ordinary magic. And it had been here all the time.

While Raeden and Dash took pictures and shared their excitement, I glanced back at the distant mountains like I had done so long ago when I'd been fourteen years old. Rather than daring the Universe to kill me, this time I kissed the tips of two fingers and saluted that horizon.

Thank you, I thought silently. *Thank you for everything.*

Mailing List/Social Media

MAILING LIST
Don't miss out on the latest news and information about all of my books. Join my Readers Group:
https://www.subscribepage.com/u0x4q3

FACEBOOK
https://www.facebook.com/todd.fahnestock

AMAZON AUTHOR PAGE
https://www.amazon.com/Todd-Fahnestock/e/B004N1MILG

ACKNOWLEDGEMENTS

There are so many people to thank for this book. Wow. From the support Dash and I had at home to the new friends we found on the trail to our wonderful cheering section on social media to our family far and near who came through for us time and again. We have so many to thank for so much.

Nancy, Robert, Mallory and Raeden – Thank you for allowing us to make your home our destination after 450 miles. For all the food and the good company. For that last-day save on the trail (Sir Robert on his metal steed!). There are just so many things. Family forever!

Chris M. – My co-worker, my one-woman writing support team. What the hell would I do without you? I'd be lost. Thank you for your penultimate scanning of the novel. And thank you, as always, for being honest.

Mandy – My Defense Against the Dark Typos Teacher. Thank you for your speedy and professional efforts on behalf of this book.

Rashed – Your generosity never ceases to inspire me. You come through for me every time. Thank you for your helping me shape the cover. It's beautiful.

Carla and Chris L. – Thank you for the loaner! Your little haven in Buena Vista became our little haven during the most important moment of the trail. You are always there for our children and for us.

Lawdon – Thanks for the great advice. I only wished I'd applied it (and the duct tape) on the first day. Puerto Rico forever! (I swear I will beat you and Tiffanny at that game someday…)

Mark – This book wouldn't exist without you. Or at least not this iteration and not so quickly. (Of course, my Fairmist fans may have a bone to pick with you, being as how I paused the 3rd in that series when this volume took over…)

A.J. – Sir, you are a gentleman and a scholar. Thank you for your enthusiasm. For going hours out of your way to walk the trail with us. For teaching my son about birds and bugs and everything else. For bringing the food and the fun. Riverview Elementary Alums forever!

Sergio, Letty and your amazing family – You picked us up at a low point and made an adventure out of a bad situation. You taught my son that strangers can be kind. We will never forget you.

Megan – Let's face it, you started all this. You are always there when I need you, through the years, through the decades. CC-mates forever!

To all of my fabulous beta readers. You really came through for me. So many great catches and such helpful feedback. Thank you!

- Katelin Barson
- Aaron Brown
- Giles Carwyn
- Lynette Conner
- Meg Dagon
- Tiffanny Hale
- Damien Kirk
- Chris Lamson
- Dave Mathewson
- Dr. Bob Mines
- Laurie Pessetto
- Kerry Wasson Quirk
- Nancy Shanks

To all the hikers and trail angels I met along the way, and most especially to River Dip, Gretchen (Fleet!), Genaro, Smiley, Jack, Bree, Paige, Jamil, Tony, Gandalf, Houdini, Candyman, Hot Mess, Seeker, TL, Doc, G-Boy, Sunburn, Specs, Gordito, and so many others. Though we only knew each of you for a short time, your collective impact was life changing.

And finally, to Brighteyes, my love. It all begins and ends with you. This life adventure was custom made for us. Let's live another hundred years.

AUTHOR LETTER

This story came as a bit of a surprise. I say a "bit" because when Dash and I reached the third week of this five-week adventure, I had already begun to think about stories involving The Colorado Trail. However, every idea I imagined was a fiction story with characters that didn't have much—or any—resemblance to Dash and me.

The idea to tell the story as it really happened only came later, at the insistence of a friend.

As I mentioned in the book, I posted a new installment of our journey every week on Facebook during Zero Days and trail breaks. I also mentioned that A.J., my good friend from elementary school, saw one of those posts and joined us on the trail for a couple days. What I didn't mention was the outpouring of support and interest from many other friends. One of these was Mark Stallings. He was excited about what we were doing, and he offered to meet us in Durango when we finished, clap us on the back and buy me a beer. That particular scenario never panned out, but when I returned to Englewood, he insisted that he and his wife take me out to dinner. So that's what we did.

As I regaled them with the true-life story over plates of Mexican food, Mark said, "Damn. This is fascinating. Are you going to write the book?"

"I've actually got two ideas," I said, and I gave him a brief synopsis of the fiction stories I had concocted.

He paused for a moment, then said, "Here's what I think you should do. Write three books. The two you just mentioned, and then the nonfiction story of your actual journey. That's what I want to read."

"Three Colorado Trail novels?"

"Definitely."

I had, of course, thought about chronicling the tale as it

had actually happened, but nonfiction wasn't really my wheelhouse, and I'd had significant problems with follow-through on nonfiction stories in the past.

But Mark's enthusiasm infected me. By the time I left the restaurant, I was ready to write three Colorado Trail books, starting with the actual account of my journey with Dash.

The next day, I went to my computer and jotted down notes. The notes turned into a scene. That scene turned into two, and I was off to the races.

Much like *Summer of the Fetch*, a fiction story I'd finished just before getting on the CT, *Ordinary Magic* flowed almost effortlessly into the keyboard. It was strangely easy because, in contrast to my fiction work where I have to completely invent every situation, I had a wealth of real-life anecdotes ready to go. All I had to do was pick and choose.

About ten chapters in, the heart of the tale began to emerge. I'd originally wanted this book to be a story about a dad bonding with his son at that critical growing-up age of fourteen. But instead it became a coming-of-age story for both of us. Dash's during the hike mixed with mine from thirty-six years ago.

As reliving the journey of the trail dredged up memories from long ago and their influence on my personality, writing this story became an adventure in itself. It took me places I never would have imagined, and it finally solidified into the book you're now holding.

Thank you for reading this, for walking the trail with me. I hope you enjoyed it. I don't imagine I'll ever write another book quite like it.

Until next time, may your life be full of adventures. And happy reading!

-Todd Fahnestock

ALSO BY TODD FAHNESTOCK

Tower of the Four Series
Episode 1 – The Quad
Episode 2 – The Tower
Episode 3 – The Test
Episode 4 – The Nightmare
Episode 5 – The Resurrection
The Champions Academy (Episodes 1-3 omnibus)

Threadweavers Series
Wildmane
The GodSpill
Threads of Amarion
God of Dragons

The Whisper Prince Series
Fairmist
The Undying Man
The Slate Wizards (Forthcoming)

Standalone Novels
Charlie Fiction
Summer of the Fetch

Short Stories
Urchin: A Tower of the Four Short Story
Royal: A Tower of the Four Short Story
Princess: A Tower of the Four Short Story
Parallel Worlds Anthology: *Threshold*
Fantastic Realms Anthology: *Ten for Every One*
Dragonlance: The Cataclysm – *Seekers*
Dragonlance: Heroes & Fools – *Songsayer*
Dragonlance: The History of Krynn – *The Letters of Trayn Minaas*

ABOUT THE AUTHOR

Todd Fahnestock is a writer of fantasy for all ages and winner of the New York Public Library's Books for the Teen Age Award. *Threadweavers* and *The Whisper Prince Trilogy* are two of his bestselling epic fantasy series. He is a 2021 finalist for the Colorado Book Award and winner of the Colorado Authors League Award for Writing Excellence for *Tower of the Four: The Champions Academy*. His passions are fantasy and his quirky, fun-loving family. When he's not writing, he teaches Taekwondo, swaps middle grade humor with his son, plays Ticket to Ride with his wife, plots creative stories with his daughter, and plays vigorously with Galahad the Weimaraner. **Visit Todd at** www.toddfahnestock.com

Made in the USA
Middletown, DE
03 March 2023